Sandro Botticelli, Filippo Lippi

Works of the Italian engravers of the fifteenth century

reproduced in facsimile by photo-intaglio

Sandro Botticelli, Filippo Lippi

Works of the Italian engravers of the fifteenth century
reproduced in facsimile by photo-intaglio

ISBN/EAN: 9783743304451

Manufactured in Europe, USA, Canada, Australia, Japa

Cover: Foto ©Thomas Meinert / pixelio.de

Manufactured and distributed by brebook publishing software
(www.brebook.com)

Sandro Botticelli, Filippo Lippi

Works of the Italian engravers of the fifteenth century

WORKS OF
THE ITALIAN ENGRAVERS

OF THE

FIFTEENTH CENTURY

REPRODUCED IN FACSIMILE BY PHOTO-INTAGLIO

WITH AN INTRODUCTION

BY

GEORGE WILLIAM REID, F.S.A.

Keeper of the Prints and Drawings in the British Museum

WITH LETTERPRESS DESCRIPTIONS OF THE WORKS ILLUSTRATED, AND COPIOUS EXTRACTS
FROM THE TEXT OF THE POEMS.

First Series – Illustrations :

IL LIBRO DEL MONTE SANCTO DI DIO, 1477; LA DIVINA COMMEDIA OF
DANTE, 1481; AND THE TRIUMPHS OF PETRARCH.

LONDON.

BERNARD QUARITCH.

1884

Printed by Spott, Printers,
Great Queen St., London, W.C.

INTRODUCTION.

THE present time may, in many respects, be considered auspicious for the publication of a series of Reproductions from the Fifteenth-century Prints of the Italian School, inasmuch as public attention has recently been, and is about to be again, called to their peculiar merits. Vicomte Henri Delaborde, of the Bibliothèque Nationale, Paris, has just published an excellent work on "La Gravure en Italie avant Marc-Antoine." Dr. Lippmann, of Berlin, is employed on the drawings of Botticelli obtained from the Hamilton Collection, with a view to explaining the connexion between them and contemporary pictures or prints. Mr. Richard Fisher has written an essay upon the Early Italian Prints in the British Museum, which will appear with the Second Volume of his Catalogue of them now in the course of compilation.

The study of early Italian prints and engravings is one which I had myself hoped to elucidate more fully; and it is with regret that I find myself now unable to accomplish the task, which I must leave to younger men. Yet, although I may not have succeeded in throwing new light on the history of Fifteenth-century Art, there is one thing in relation to it which I may, I hope, fairly take credit for having done, viz., that, having had constantly such an object in view, I have prepared the way for future study by bringing together all that is essential as a basis for further work, not only by investigating and obtaining such unique and rare prints of the early Italian School as came in my way from time to time, but by purchasing whole series of prints, and what are generally termed "Galleries," for the British Museum. These have now been arranged in Schools in chronological order. Besides this, I have secured almost all the reproductions from drawings made by M. Braun and others, so that the student now has in the Print Room of the Museum facilities for research which previously were not within his reach there, and such as cannot be obtained elsewhere.

Another advantage which I may claim to have procured for the student is this, that one section of my Catalogue of the Print Room, now in course of preparation, is devoted to "Subjects," on the principle employed to a limited extent by Zani, in his "Enciclopedia Metodica" (1819-1822). With an old print or drawing before him, representing, say, the Death of Samson, the student can in a few minutes have all the engravings of that subject placed before him. Such an arrangement as this will be found useful in several ways, and will certainly facilitate the identification of pictures with prints after them or drawings made for their preparation.

ILLUSTRATIONS OF "IL LIBRO DEL MONTE SANCTO DI DIO."

In 1477 there was published at Florence a small folio volume, which commences at folio 4 thus: ". . . Monte Sancto di Dio composto da Messer Antonio da Siena Reverendissimo Veschovo di Fuligno"; and ends :—" Finito el mõte sõo di dio pũe Nicolo di lorëzo della magna Florentie X., Die Mensis Septembris, ANNO DOMINI. M.CCCCLXXVII." The writer was Antonio Bettini. The work consists of three treatises on the "Mount of Christ," the "Glory of Paradise," and the "Punishments of Hell," which form the subject of the three engravings contained in the volume and here reproduced. They are from designs of Botticelli, and generally regarded as having been also engraved by him.

ILLUSTRATIONS OF THE "DIVINA COMMEDIA" OF DANTE ALIGHIERI.

"La Divina Commedia," or, as it is called, the "Vision of Dante," consists of three parts, treating of Hell, Purgatory, and Paradise. The first of these, Hell, forms the subject illustrated by the prints here reproduced. They consist of nineteen vignettes (and one repetition of the third) illustrating the first nineteen cantos of the poem, the "Inferno." The first issue of the work at Florence in 1481, printed by Nicolo di Lorenzo della Magna (Nicholas of Breslau), contained only two of the illustrations, those to the first and second cantos, the others not being ready at the time; but in a subsequent issue seventeen others were added, making up the whole nineteen. A volume containing the complete series of the nineteen prints is very rare.

The collection of the Print Department of the British Museum contains a very fine set of these prints, with the rare repetition of No. 3, and there are also in the Library of that Institution six fine copies of the work, two with the complete series, one in the Grenville Library, being without the Roman numerals, which were afterwards engraved on the plates. Another copy in the Cracherode Collection contains eight of the prints, one being in duplicate; six of these are also in the first state before the numerals. There are two copies, one with the two illustrations to the 1st and 2nd Cantos, and the other with only one illustration—that to Canto 2.

The reproductions now presented to the public have been taken from the best prints in the collection in the British Museum, those of the Dante series comprising examples chosen from among seven copies of the work.

The prints have been described by Bartsch, Ottley, Passavant, and Koloff. There is a difference of opinion amongst them as to whether Sandro Botticelli, by whom they were unquestionably designed, had any hand in the engraving, and, if he had, to what extent, or whether he was only the designer, and Baccio Baldini alone was the engraver. More recent investigations of the subject and comparisons with other works of Botticelli, especially a collection of the original drawings by him illustrating the whole of the "Divina Commedia" of Dante recently acquired by the Prussian Government, have led to the opinion that these vignettes were only designed by Botticelli, and were engraved (possibly under his direction) by Baldini, of whose style of work they bear indubitable signs.

ILLUSTRATIONS OF THE TRIUMPHS OF PETRARCH.

In the six poems entitled the "Triumphs of Love," "Chastity," "Death," "Fame," "Time," and "Eternity" Petrarch describes the six states of Man.

The nature of man being composed of passion and reason, he at the commencement of life gives himself up to the delights and pleasures of the senses, understood under the name of Love. In the second state man overcomes Love by Reason, and Chastity (personified by Laura) triumphs over Love. In the third the poet explains the triumph of Death, in that it deprives man of his vital functions. In the fourth he shows that Fame triumphs over Death, in that good deeds never die, but live in the memory of posterity. In the fifth Time triumphs over Fame, in that the glory of the world ends with years. In the sixth at last Eternity triumphs over Time and conducts man to Heaven, where he enjoys the blessedness which is there the final state.

This set of prints, illustrating the Triumphs of Petrarch, has erroneously been attributed to Nicoletto da Modena, by Bartsch, but it is more likely that they were designed, if not executed, by Fra Filippo Lippi. They have many salient characteristics of his style and treatment. If this supposition be correct, it was of importance that the nation should possess a set of them having all their simplicity and chasteness. They were inserted and bound in an imperfect copy of the edition of Petrarch,—"I Triumphi col comenti di B. Glicino Finisse il commento delli triumphi del Petrarcha composto pas il prestantissimo philosoppo Messa Bernardo da Monte Mecinio da Scina. Impresso in Venetia con grado diligentia per Bernardino da Novara nelli anni del nostro Signore MCCCCLXXXVIII. adi. xviii. Aprile," which has its own woodcut illustrations, the inserted plates never having any text issued with them.

Having been executed on a very soft metal, probably silver or unhammered copper, the plates had begun to wear from the effects of taking even so few as half a dozen impressions, and consequently, to supply a very limited demand, they had to be reworked. This latter operation, as in many similar instances, was evidently carried out by an engraver of inferior skill. But the plates from which these specimens have been taken were, without doubt, in all their original purity just as they left the artist's hands, and the impressions themselves, from their having been inserted in a book, have been preserved without a blemish. A duplicate set of these six Triumphs is in the British Museum, printed from the plates after some re-engraving of them had taken place, which we must regard as second states, since still later ones are known to exist.

The six prints in the first states from which these reproductions are taken were inserted and bound in a folio edition of " I Triumphi " which formerly belonged to the library of the Earl of Sunderland, and which was removed from Blenheim, and sold by auction in London in 1882. The volume with the inserted prints was bought after the sale for the British Museum, by special Parliamentary grant, for £2,050.

The acquisition of an example of these rare prints in any state is an event to be noted in a life-time ; but the opportunity of obtaining a perfect set, evidently issued together, and in the purest state and condition, was, it must be admitted, a sufficient warrant for the Trustees of the British Museum to recommend its purchase to the Treasury.

As a means of explaining the subjects illustrated in the prints of which reproductions are here presented to the Public, it has been thought the best and simplest course to give opposite each print a concise description of the part of the work depicted, and such extracts from the text of the poets as will sufficiently explain the illustrations.

The reproductions, I am pleased to state, have been most successfully executed by Messrs. Dawson.

G. W. R.

LIST OF PLATES.

IL LIBRO DEL MONTE SANCTO DI DIO.

I.

THE Author, in three separate treatises, the "Mount of Christ," the "Glory of Paradise," and the "Punishment of Hell," teaches what should be the highest aim and perfect end of the faithful Christian,—how he may by various degrees attain to the summit of Glory in Paradise. His ascent thereto is allegorically represented as by a ladder placed firmly in the ground of wide-spread Knowledge and Humility, and reaching up to the triple mount, Faith, Hope, and Charity, on the summit of which stands his Saviour. This ladder is called Perseverance, one of its sides being called Prayer and the other Sacrament. It has eleven steps,—the first, Prudence ; the second, Temperance ; the third, Fortitude ; the fourth, Justice ; the fifth, Fear ; the sixth, Piety ; the seventh, Knowledge ; the eighth, Fortitude ;* the ninth, Counsel ; the tenth, Intellect ; and the eleventh, Wisdom. Man, knowing his own weakness and feeling himself held back by Blindness (Cecita), raises his eyes to the sublime height whence alone help can come, and, having no confidence in his own strength, says,—" I will lift up mine eyes unto the hills, from whence cometh my help. My help cometh from the Lord." He then proceeds to mount the steps of the ladder ; ascends the first four, Prudence, Temperance, Fortitude, and Justice ; and by the exercise of these four virtues he elevates himself to that height at which he may become as nearly perfect as possible for him to be ; but the height of the mountain to which the ladder leads being supernatural and above the heavens, it is necessary for the earnest Christian to be drawn up by the Divine help, and thus see God the King of Glory. To him who has already ascended the first four steps God grants the Holy Spirit, which facilitates his ascent of the remaining seven, making the whole eleven.

---

* Fortitude occurs a second time, it forming the third and eighth steps of the ladder.

IL LIBRO DEL MONTE SANCTO DI DIO.

II.

In the second treatise the "Glory of Paradise" is then treated upon by the author, and is illustrated by a full-length figure of Jesus Christ standing in one of the almond-shaped glories (*mandorla*) in which the Italian painters, and in general the artists of the fourteenth and fifteenth centuries, were accustomed to surround the image of the Saviour.

IL LIBRO DEL MONTE SANCTO DI DIO.

III.

In the third treatise the Punishments of Hell are treated on. They are described as mental sufferings, corporal pain, and eternal torment in fire within the bowels of the earth. The author does not describe the various kinds of horrible tortures depicted as being inflicted by demons in the print, which are mainly those adapted from the fresco of Hell executed in the fourteenth century by Bernardo Orcagna, still in existence in the Campo Santo at Pisa.

DANTE'S INFERNO—CANTO I.

Dante loses himself at night in a gloomy wood, and at daybreak, reaching the foot of a mountain, in attempting its ascent is molested by a panther, a lion, and a wolf. He then meets the spirit of Virgil, who tells him, if he will follow, he will show him the punishments of Hell and Purgatory, and be afterwards conducted by a worthier spirit (Beatrice) into Paradise. Virgil moves on, Dante following him :—

I found me in a gloomy wood astray,
Gone from the path direct : and e'en to tell
It were no easy task, how savage wild
That forest, how robust its growth.

*   *   *   *

But when a mountain's foot I reach'd, where closed
The valley that had pierced my heart with dread,
I look'd aloft, and saw his shoulders broad
Already vested with that planet's beam
Who leads all wand'rers safe through ev'ry way.

*   *   *   *

Scarce the ascent
Began, when, lo ! a panther, nimble, light,
And cover'd with a speckled skin, appear'd ;
Nor, when it saw me, vanish'd ; rather strove
To check my onward going ; that ofttimes
With purpose to retrace my steps, I turn'd.

*   *   *   *

And by new dread succeeded, when in view
A lion came 'gainst me as it appear'd,
With his head held aloft and hunger-mad,

That e'en the air was fear struck. A she-wolf
Was at his heels.

*   *   *   *

While to the lower space with backward step
I fell, my ken discern'd the form of one
Whose voice seem'd faint through long disuse of speech
When him in that great desert I espied,
" Have mercy on me," cried I out aloud,
" Spirit ! or living man ! whate'er thou be "
He answer'd : " Now not man, man once I was."

*   *   *   *

" I, for thy profit pond'ring, now devise
That thou mayst follow me ; and I, thy guide,
Will lead thee hence through an eternal space,
Where thou shalt hear despairing shrieks and see
Spirits of old tormented, who invoke
A second death ; and those next view, who dwell
Content in fire, for that they hope to come,
Whene'er the time may be, among the blest,
Into whose regions, if thou them desire
To ascend, a spirit worthier than I
Must lead thee, in whose charge when I depart
Thou shalt be left."

CANTO II.

Dante distrusts his own strength unaided being sufficient for undertaking the proposed journey. Virgil encourages him, and relates how Beatrice had appeared to him and besought him to assist Dante. His courage becomes restored, and he begs Virgil to lead on, and he will follow his guide, master, and lord :—

" Myself I deem not worthy, and none else
Will deem me. I, if on this voyage, then,
I venture, fear it will in folly end.
Thou, who art wise, better my meaning know'st
Than I can speak."

*   *   " If right thy words
I scan," replied that shade magnanimous,
" Thy soul is by vile fear assail'd, which oft
So overcasts a man that he recoils
From noblest resolution, like a beast
At some false semblance in the twilight gloom.
That from this terror thou mayst free thyself,
I will instruct thee why I came, and what
I heard in that same instant, when for thee
Grief touch'd me first. I was among the tribe
Who rest suspended, when a dame, so blest
And lovely I besought her to command,
Call'd me ; her eyes were brighter than the star
Of day ; and she, with gentle voice and soft
Angelically tuned, her speech address'd :
' O courteous shade of Mantua ! thou whose fame
Yet lives and shall live long as nature lasts !
A friend not of my fortune but myself
On the wide desert on his road has met
Hindrance so great, that he through fear has turn'd.
Now, much I dread lest he past help have stray'd,

And I be risen too late for his relief,
From what in heaven of him I heard. Speed now,
And by thy eloquent persuasive tongue,
And by all means for his deliverance meet,
Assist him. So to me will comfort spring.
I who now bid thee on this errand forth
Am Beatrice !'

*   *   *   *

When she had ended her bright beaming eyes
Tearful she turn'd aside ; whereat I felt
Redoubled zeal to serve thee. As she will'd
Thus am I come."

*   *   *   *

As florets, by the frosty air of night
Bent down and closed when day has blanch'd their leaves,
Rise all unfolded on their spiry stems ;
So was my fainting vigour new-restored,
And to my heart such kindly courage ran,
That I as one undaunted soon replied :
" O full of pity she, who undertook
My succour ! and thou kind, who didst perform
So soon her true behest ! With such desire
Thou has disposed me to renew my voyage,
That my first purpose fully is resumed.
Lead on : one only will is in us both.
Thou art my guide, my master thou, and lord."

DANTE'S INFERNO—CANTO III.

DANTE follows Virgil to the gate of Hell, on which the former reads the terrible inscription. Led by Virgil, Dante enters the portal. He then beholds a throng of spirits, who rend the air with groans, cries, and lamentations. The pair then pass on to the river Acheron, where they find the ferryman Charon, who conveys the spirits across it. Dante, overcome by fear and terror at what he sees, falls down senseless as if in sleep :—

" Through me you pass into the city of woe ;
Through me you pass into eternal pain .
Through me, amongst the people lost for aye.
Justice the founder of my fabric moved.
To rear me was the task of power divine,
Supremest wisdom and primeval love,
Before me things create were none, save things
Eternal, and eternal I endure.
All hope abandon, ye who enter here !"

*　　*　　*　　*　　*

Here sighs, with lamentations and loud moans,
Resounded through the air pierced by no star,
That e'en I wept at ent'ring.　*　　*
I then : "Master, what doth aggrieve them thus
That they lament so loud ?"　He straight replied,
" That will I tell thee briefly. These of death
No hope may entertain ; and their blind life
So meanly passes, that all other lots
They envy. Fame of them the world hath none,
Nor suffers ; Mercy and Justice scorn them both.
Speak not of them, but look and pass them by."
And I, who straightway look'd, beheld a flag,
Which whirling ran around so rapidly,
That it no pause obtain'd ; and following came
Such a long train of spirits, I should ne'er

Have thought that death so many had despoil'd.

*　　*　　*　　*　　*

Till we had reach'd the river, I from speech
Abstain'd. And, lo ! towards us in a bark
Comes on an old man, hoary white with eld,
Crying, "Woe to you, wicked spirits ! hope not
Ever to see the sky again. I come
To take you to the other shore, across
Into eternal darkness, there to dwell
In fierce heat and in ice　*　　*　　*
Then all together, sorely wailing, drew
To the cursed strand, that every man must pass
Who fears not God. Charon, demoniac form,
With eyes of burning coal, collects them all,
Beck'ning, and each that lingers with his oar
Strikes.　*　　*　　*　　*
Thus go they over through the umber'd wave,
And ever they on the opposing bank
Be landed, on this side another throng
Still gathers.　*　　*　　*
Fear chills my brow. The sad earth gave a blast,
That, light'ning, shot forth a vermilion flame,
Which all my senses conquer'd quite, and I
Down dropp'd as one with sudden slumber seized.

CANTO III A.

REPETITION varying, as will be seen, materially in the design from the last, and not belonging to the set ; it is, however, placed by Bartsch at the end of the series. William Young Ottley appears to be of an opinion that this composition was designed and engraved by another hand, and no doubt he is perfectly correct.

DANTE'S INFERNO—CANTO IV.

A HEAVY clap of thunder rouses Dante from the swoon into which he has fallen. Following Virgil, he descends into Limbo, the first circle of Hell, the abode of those who, though not sinners, have not been baptised; amongst these he meets many men of great renown,—Homer, Horace, Ovid, Lucan. These, beckoning him, lead him on to a magnificent castle, begirt by seven lofty walls enclosing a verdant mead, where he is shown many great spirits of antiquity. His guide then leads him into the second circle of Hell :—

Broke the deep slumber in my brain a crash
Of heavy thunder, that I shook myself,
As one by main force roused.

  *   *   *

"Now let us to the blind world there beneath
Descend," the bard began, all pale of look,
  *   *   * Onward, this said, he moved,
And, ent'ring, led me with him, on the bounds
Of the first circle that surrounds th' abyss
Here, as mine ear could note, no plaint was heard
Except of sighs, that made th' eternal air
Tremble, not caused by tortures, but from grief
Felt by those multitudes, many and vast,
Of men, women, and infants. Then to me
The gentle guide : " Inquirest thou not what spirits
Are these which thou behold'st ? Ere thou pass
Farther, I would thou know that these of sin
Were blameless ; and, if aught they merited,
It profits not, since baptism was not theirs,
The portal to thy faith. If they before
The Gospel lived, they served not God aright ;
And among such am I. For these defects,
And for no other evil, we are lost,
Only so far afflicted that we live
Desiring without hope."   *   *

Meantime a voice I heard : " Honour the bard
Sublime ! his shade returns that left us late."
No sooner ceased the sound than I beheld
Four mighty spirits towards us bend their steps,
Of semblance neither sorrowful nor glad.
When thus my master kind began : " Mark him,
Who in his right hand bears that falchion 'keen,
The other three preceding, as their lord.
This is that Homer of all bards supreme ;
Flaccus the next, in Satire's vein excelling ;
The third is Naso ; Lucan is the last."
  *   *   * At foot
Of a magnificent castle we arrived,
Seven times with lofty walls begirt, and round,
Defended by a pleasant stream. O'er this
As o'er dry land we pass'd. Next through seven gates
I with those sages enter'd, and we came
Into a mead with lively verdure fresh.

  *   *   *

We to one side retired, into a place
Open and bright and lofty, whence each one
Stood manifest to view. Incontinent,
There on the green enamel of the plain
Were shown me the great spirits, by whose sight
I am exalted in my own esteem.

CANTO V.

DESCENDING into the second circle, Dante encounters at the entrance Minos, the judge of the Infernal Regions, who bids him beware entering lest harm come to him. There he beholds the punishments of carnal sinners who are incessantly blown about by violent winds in darkness, among whom he sees the spirits of Semiramis, Cleopatra, Achilles, Helen, Paris, and others. Seeing Francesca de Rimini, and her lover Malatesta, she relates her sad love-story, which so overpowers his feelings that he faints :—

From the first circle I descended thus
Down to the second, which, a lesser space
Embracing, so much more of grief contains,
Provoking bitter means. There Minos stands,
Grinning with ghastly feature ; he, of all
Who enter, strict examining the crimes,
Gives sentence, and dismisses them beneath,
According as he foldeth him around :
For, when before him comes th' ill-fated soul,
It all confesses ; and that judge severe
Of sins, considering what place in hell
Suits the transgression, with his tail so oft
Himself encircles, as degrees beneath
He dooms it to descend. Before him stand
Alway a numerous throng ; and in his turn
Each one, to judgment passing, speaks, and hears
His fate, thence downward to his dwelling hurl'd.
  *   *   *
            Into a place I came
Where light was silent all. Bellowing there groan'd
A noise as of a sea in tempest torn
By warring winds. The stormy blast of Hell

With restless fury drives the spirits on,
Whirl'd round and dash'd amain with sore annoy.

  *   *   *

When I had heard my sage instructor name
Those dames and knights of antique days, o'erpower'd
By pity, well-nigh in amaze my mind
Was lost ; and I began : " Bard ! willingly
I would address those two together coming,
Which seem so light before the wind." He thus :
" Note thou, when near they to us approach ;
Then by that love which carries them along,
Entreat, and they will come." Soon as the wind
Sway'd them towards us, I thus framed my speech :
" O wearied spirits ! come and hold discourse
With us if by none else restrain'd." As doves,
By fond desire invited, on wide wings
And firm, to their sweet nest returning home,
Cleave the air, wafted by their will along,
Thus, issued from that troop where Dido ranks,
They, through the ill air speeding, with such force
My cry prevail'd, by strong affection urged.

DANTE'S INFERNO—CANTO VI.

RECOVERING from his insensibility, Dante arrives in the third circle, and finds himself in the midst of souls tormented for gluttony by ceaseless showers of hailstones, sleet, and discoloured foul water pouring on them. He sees Cerberus, the cruel three-headed monster, flaying and tearing the limbs of his victims in pieces with his claws. A noted glutton called Ciacco tells Dante of the discord that will happen at Florence. Passing on, discoursing with his guide, he comes to the fourth circle, where he meets Plutus:—

My sense reviving, that erewhile had droop'd
With pity for the kindred shades, whence grief
O'ercame me wholly, straight around I see
New torments, new tormented souls, which way
Soe'er I move, or turn, or bend my sight.
In the third circle I arrive, of showers
Ceaseless, accursed, heavy and cold, unchanged
For ever, both in kind and in degree.
Large hail discolour'd water, sleety flow
Through the dun midnight air stream'd down amain,
Stank all the land whereon that tempest fell.
Cerberus, cruel monster, fierce and strange,
Through his wide threefold throat, barks as a dog
Over the multitude immersed beneath.
His eyes glare crimson, black his unctuous beard,
His belly large, and claw'd the hands, with which
He tears the spirits, flays them, and their limbs
Piecemeal disparts. Howling, there spread, as curs,
Under the rainy deluge, with one side
The other screening, oft they roll them round,
A wretched, godless crew. When that great worm
Descried us savage Cerberus, he oped

His jaws, and the fangs show'd us ; not a limb
Of him but trembled. Then my guide, his palms
Expanding on the ground, thence fill'd with earth
Raised them, and cast it in his ravenous maw.
E'en as a dog, that yelling bays for food
His keeper, when the morsel comes, lets fall
His fury, bent alone with eager haste
To swallow it ; so dropp'd the loathsome cheeks
Of demon Cerberus, who thundering stuns
The spirits, that they for deafness wish in vain.

*   *   *   *   *

"Inform me
Who thou art, that in a place so sad
Art set, and in such torment, that, although
Other be greater, none disgusteth more."

*   *   *   *   *

"Ye citizens
Were wont to name me Ciacco. For the sin
Of gluttony, damn'd vice, beneath this rain
E'en as thou see'st, I with fatigue am worn ;
Nor I sole spirit in this woe , all these
Have by like crime incurr'd like punishment."

CANTO VII.

DANTE encounters Plutus, who, rebuked by Virgil, falls back, and they, passing on, descend to the fourth circle, where they see the prodigal and avaricious, amongst whom are Popes, Cardinals, Kings, &c., suffering the punishment assigned them, namely, pushing weights with their breasts against each other ; then crossing the fifth circle, descending to the Stygian lake, in whose filthy waters the angry are tormented. Afterwards they arrive at the base of a tower :—

"Ah me ! O Satan ! Satan !" loud exclaim'd
Plutus, in accent hoarse of wild alarm.
And the kind sage, whom no event surprised,
To comfort me thus spake : " Let not thy fear
Harm thee, for power in him, be sure, is none
To hinder down this rock thy safe descent."
Then to that swoln lip turning. " Peace ! " he cried,
" Cursed wolf ! thy fury inward on thyself
Prey and consume thee ! Through the dark profound,
Not without cause, he passes. So 'tis will'd
On high."
As sails, full-spread and bellying with the wind,
Drop suddenly collapsed if the mast split,
So to the ground down dropp'd the cruel fiend.
Thus we, descending to the fourth steep ledge,
Goin'd on the dismal shore, that all the woe
Hems in of all the universe *   *
New pains, new troubles, as I here beheld
Wherefore doth fault of ours bring us to this?
E'en as a billow on Charybdis rising,
Against encounter'd billow dashing breaks,

Such is the dance this wretched race must lead,
Whom more than elsewhere numerous here I found.
From one side and the other, with loud voice,
Both roll'd on weights, by main force of their breasts,
Then smote together, and each one forthwith
Roll'd them back voluble, turning again ;
Exclaiming these, " Why hold'st thou so fast ? "
Those answering, " And why castest thou away ? "
So, still repeating their despiteful song,
They to the opposite point, on either hand,
Traversed the horrid circle ; then arrived,
Both turn'd them round, and through the middle space
Conflicting met again. *   *
*   *   We the circle cross'd
To the next steep, arriving at a well,
That boiling pours itself down to a fons
Sluiced from its source. Far murkier was the wave
Than sablest grain : and we in company
Of the inky waters, journeying by their side,
Enter'd, though by a different track, beneath
Into a lake, the Stygian named.

PHLEGYAS, the ferryman of the lake, summoned by the signal of two cressets, comes in his bark towards Dante and Virgil. They step into the vessel, and are rowed along the miry stream, on their way meeting with the spirit of Filippo Argenti, who, stretching forth his hands to them, is thrust back by Virgil. Arriving at the city of Dis, they find its gates closed against them by Demons, which angers Virgil :—

My theme pursuing, I relate that ere
We reach'd the lofty turret's base, our eyes
Its height ascended, where we mark'd unhung
Two cressets, and another saw from far
Return the signal.   *   *   *
   *   *   *
Never was arrow from the cord dismiss'd
That ran its way so nimbly through the air,
As a small bark, that through the waves I spied
Toward us coming, under the sole sway
Of one that ferried it, who cried aloud :
"Art thou arrived, fell spirit?" "Phlegyas, Phlegyas,
This time thou criest in vain," my lord replied ;
"No longer shalt thou have us, but while o'er
The slimy pool we pass."
   *   My guide, descending, stepp'd
Into the skiff, and bade me enter next,
Close at his side ; nor till my entrance seem'd
The vessel freighted. Soon as both embark'd,
Cutting the waves, goes on the ancient prow,
More deeply than with others it is wont.
While we our course o'er the dead channel held,
One drench'd in mire before me came, and said :
"Who art thou that thus comest ere thine hour?"

I answer'd : "Though I come, I tarry not ;
But who art thou that art become so foul?"
"One as thou see'st who mourns," he straight replied.
To which I thus : "In mourning and in woe,
Cursed spirit, tarry thou. I know thee well
E'en thus in filth disguised." Then stretch'd he forth
Hands to the bark ; whereof my teacher sage
Aware, thrusting him back : "Away, down there,
To the other dogs !"   *   *   *
And thus the good instructor : "Now my son
Draws near the city that of Dis is named,
With its grave denizens, a mighty throng."
   *   *   *   *
We came within the fosses deep that moat
This region comfortless. The walls appear'd
As they were framed of iron.   *   *
   *   Upon the gates I spied
More than a thousand who of old from heaven
Were shower'd. With ireful gestures, "Who is this,"
They cried, "that, without death first felt, goes through
The regions of the dead?"   *   *
   *   *   Closed were the gates,
By those our adversaries, on the breast
Of my liege lord.

CANTO IX.

DANTE beholds at top of a tower the three Furies enveloped in flames, who call upon Medusa to change him to stone. Lest this should happen by Dante's viewing her, Virgil covers with his hands the eyes of Dante. An angel then appears gliding over the lake, who with a touch of a wand causes the gates to open. Entering the city, they come where heretics are suffering the punishments allotted them in sepulchres of fire :—

   *   *   Mine eye toward the lofty tower
Had drawn me wholly to its burning top,
Where in an instant I beheld uprisen
At once three hellish Furies, stain'd with blood.
In limb and motion feminine they seem'd ;
Around them greenest Hydras twisting roll'd
Their volumes ; adders and cerastes crept
Instead of hair, and their fierce temples bound.
   *   *   *   *
Their breast they each one clawing tore ; themselves
Smote with their palms, and such shrill clamour raised,
That to the bard I clung, suspicion-bound.
"Hasten, Medusa ; so to adamant
Him shall we change ;" all, looking down, exclaim'd :
"E'en whom by Theseus' might assail'd, we took
No ill revenge." "Turn thyself round and keep
Thy countenance hid ; for, if the Gorgon dire
Be shown, and thou shouldst view it, thy return
Upwards would be for ever lost." This said,
Himself, my gentle master, turn'd me round ;

Nor trusted he my hands, but with his own
He also hid me.   *   *   *
Mine eyes he loosed, and spake : "And now direct
Thy visual nerve along that ancient foam,
There thickest where the smoke ascends." As frogs
Before their foe, the serpent, through the wave
Fly swiftly all, till at the ground each one
Lies on a heap ; more than a thousand spirits
Destroy'd, so saw I fleeing before one
Who pass'd with unwet feet the Stygian sound.
He, from his face removing the gross air,
Oft his left hand forth stretch'd, and seem'd alone
By that annoyance wearied. I perceived
That he was sent from Heaven ; and to my guide
Turn'd me, who signal made that I should stand
Quiet, and bend to him. Ah, me ! how full
Of noble anger seem'd he. To the gate
He came, and with his wand touch'd it, whereat
Open without impediment it flew.

DANTE'S INFERNO—CANTO X.

Having entered the gate, and proceeding by a secret path, Dante and his guide enter the region where heretics are undergoing torments in burning sepulchres. Dante discourses with Farinata degli Uberti and Cavalcante Cavalcanti, lying in their fiery tombs. The former predicts Dante's exile. Leaving this region, they pass by a path through a noisome valley :—

I, soon as enter'd, throw mine eye around,
And see, on every part, wide-stretching space,
Replete with bitter pain and torment ill.
*   *   *   *   *
The place is all thick-spread with sepulchres;
So was it here, save what in horror here
Excell'd; for midst the graves were scatter'd flames,
Wherewith intensely all throughout they burn'd,
That iron for no craft there hotter needs.
*   *   *   *   *
"Lo! Farinata there, who hath himself
Uplifted; from his girdle upwards, all
Exposed, behold him."
*   *   *   *   *
Then, peering forth from the unclosed jaw,
Rose from his side a shade, high as the chin,
Leaning, methought, upon its knees upraised.
It look'd around, as eager to explore
If there were other with me; but, perceiving

That fond imagination quench'd, with tears
Thus spake: "If thou through this blind prison goest,
Led by thy lofty genius and profound,
Where is my son? and wherefore not with thee?"
I straight replied: "Not of myself I come;
By him who there expects me, through this clime
Conducted, whom perchance Guido thy son
Had in contempt." *   *   *
*   *   *   *
Meanwhile the other, great of soul, near whom
I yet was station'd, changed not count'nance stern,
Nor moved the neck, nor bent his ribbèd side.
"And if," continuing the first discourse,
"They in this art," he cried, "small skill have shown,
That doth torment me more e'en than this bed.
But not yet fifty times shall be relumed
Her aspect, who reigns here Queen of this realm
Ere thou shalt know the full weight of that art."
*   *   *   *

CANTO XI.

Dante and Virgil come to the verge of a high bank surrounded by craggy rocks which encloses the seventh circle. Dante marks a sepulchre bearing a scroll with the words upon it, "I have in charge Pope Anastasius, whom Photinus drew from the right path." Both retiring behind the lid of this tomb, to avoid the fetid exhalations rising from the abyss, Virgil instructs Dante as to the disposition of the three following circles, and as to what sinners are therein punished, and, after discoursing on other subjects, they pass on to a steep passage leading towards the seventh circle :—

Upon the utmost verge of a high bank,
By craggy rocks environ'd round, we came,
Where woes beneath, more cruel yet, were stow'd:
And here, to shun the horrible excess
Of fetid exhalation upward cast
From the profound abyss, behind the lid
Of a great monument we stood retired,
Whereon this scroll I mark'd: "I have in charge
Pope Anastasius, whom Photinus drew
From the right path."—"Ere our descent, behoves
We make delay, that somewhat first the sense,
To the dire breath accustom'd, afterward
Regard it not." My master thus; to whom,
Answering, I spake: "Some compensation find,
That the time pass not wholly lost." He then:

"Lo! how my thoughts e'en to thy wishes tend.
My son! Within these rocks," he thus began,
"Are three close circles in gradation placed,
To these which now thou leav'st. Each one is full
Of spirits accursed; but, that the sight alone
Hereafter may suffice thee, listen how
And for what cause in durance they abide."
*   *   *   *   *
*   *   * "But follow now
My steps on forward journey bent; for now
The Fishes play with undulating glance
Along the horizon, and the Wain lies all
O'er the north-west; and onward there a space
Is our steep passage down the rocky height."

X.

DANTE'S INFERNO—CANTO XII.

DANTE and his guide descend the precipice by a rough craggy way to the seventh circle. Encountering the Minotaur, Virgil bids him stand aside, and they descend to the river of blood, wherein are immersed those who have injured others by violence, at whom Centaurs, running along the banks, aim arrows, if they attempt to emerge from it. Being opposed by three of these,—Chiron, Nessus, and Pholus,—Virgil prevails on Nessus to carry Dante across the stream :—

The place, where to descend the precipice
We came, was rough as Alp ; and on its verge
Such object lay as every eye would shun.

     *   *   *   *

At point of the disparted ridge lay stretch'd
The infamy of Crete, detested brood
Of the feign'd heifer : and, at sight of us,
It gnaw'd itself, as one with rage distract.
To him my guide exclaim'd : "Perchance thou deem'st
The King of Athens here, who, in the world
Above, thy death contrived. Monster avaunt !
He comes not tutor'd by thy sister's art,
But to behold your torments is he come."

     *   *   *   *

"But fix thine eyes beneath : the river of blood
Approaches, in which all those are steep'd
Who have by violence injured."   *
                     I beheld
An ample fosse, that in a bow was bent,
As circling all the plain ; for so my guide
Had told. Between it and the ramparts' base,
On trail ran Centaurs, with keen arrows arm'd
As in the chase they on the earth were wont.
At seeing us descend they each one stood ;

And, issuing from the troop, three sped with bows
And missile weapons chosen first   *   *
Then me he touch'd and spake : "Nessus is this,
Who for the fair Dejanira died,
And wrought himself revenge for his own fate.
He in the midst, that on his breast looks down,
Is the great Chiron who Achilles nursed ;
That other Pholus prone to wrath." Around
The fosse these go by thousands, aiming shafts
At whatsoever spirit dares emerge
From out the blood, more than his guilt allows.

     *   *   *   *

"To tread so wild a path, grant us, I pray,
One of thy band, whom we may trust secure,
Who to the ford may lead us, and convey
Across him mounted on his back ; for he
Is not a spirit that may walk the air."
Then, on his right breast turning, Chiron thus
To Nessus spake : "Return and be their guide,
And if ye chance to cross another troop,
Command them keep aloof." Onward we moved,
The faithful escort by our side, along
The border of the crimson-seething flood,
Whence, from those steep'd within, loud shrieks arose.

CANTO XIII.

THEY then enter on a forest without a path, full of knotted trees covered with poisoned thorns, in which the Harpies build their nests. In these gnarled trunks are shut up the spirits of those who have done themselves violence,—among them Piero delle Vigne, Lano, and Giacomo St. Andrea. Dante tears off a branch from one of the trees, which evokes reproaches from it. Certain black female mastiffs tear the branches which contain the spirit of St. Andrea, the fragments of which Dante, at his request, gathers up :—

We enter'd on a forest, where no track
Of steps had worn a way. Not verdant there
The foliage, but of dusky hue ; not light
The boughs and tapering, but with knares deform'd
And matted thick : fruits there were none, but thorns
Instead, with venom fill'd.   *   *
Here the brute Harpies make their nest, the same
Who from Strophades the Trojan band
Drove with dire boding of their future woe.
Broad are their pennons, of the human form
Their neck and countenance, arm'd with talons keen.
The feet and the huge belly fledged with wings.
These sit and wail on the drear mystic wood.

     *   *   *   *

                On all sides
I heard sad plainings breathe, and none could see
From whom they might have issued. In amaze
Fast bound I stood. He, as it seem'd, believed
That I had thought so many voices came
From some amid those thickets close conceal'd,
And thus his speech resumed : "If thou lop off
A single twig from one of those ill plants,
The thought thou hast conceived shall vanish quite."

Thereat, a little stretching forth my hand,
From a great wilding gather'd I a branch,
And straight the trunk exclaim'd : "Why pluck'st thou me ? '
Then, as the dark blood trickled down its side,
These words it added : "Wherefore tear'st me thus ?
Is there no touch of mercy in thy breast ?
Men once were we, that now are rooted here.
Thy hand might well have spared us, had we been
The souls of serpents."   *   *
     *   * Behind them was a wood
Full of black female mastiffs, gaunt and fleet
As greyhounds that have newly slipp'd the leash.
On him, who squatted down, they struck their fangs,
And, having rent him piecemeal, bore away
The tortured limbs.   *   *
     *   * My master spake :
"Say, who wast thou, that at so many points
Breath'st out with blood thy lamentable speech ?"
He answer'd : "O ye spirits ! arrived in time
To spy the shameful havoc that from me
My leaves hath sever'd thus, gather them up,
And at the foot of their sad parent-tree
Carefully lay them."

DANTE'S INFERNO—CANTO XIV.

DANTE and Virgil then enter on a plain of dry hot sand, wherein they see flocks of naked spirits being tormented by flakes of fire continually showering down upon them. Here they see King Capaneus, who, lying recumbent, as if in defiant dignity, addresses them. They, passing on, come to a streamlet of blood running through the sandy plain :—

A plain we reach'd, that from its sterile bed
Each plant repell'd. The mournful wood waves round
Its garland on all sides, as round the wood
Spreads the sad fosse. There, on the very edge,
Out steps we stay'd. It was an area wide
Of arid sand and thick.   *   *   *
Of naked spirits many a flock I saw,
All weeping piteously, to different laws
Subjected ; for on the earth some lay supine,
Some crouching close were seated, others paced
Incessantly around ; the latter tribe
More numerous, those fewer who beneath
The torment lay, but louder in their grief
O'er all the sand fell slowly, wafting down
Dilated flakes of fire,   *   *   *
So fell the eternal fiery flood, wherewith
The marle glow'd underneath,   *   *
Unceasing was the play of wretched hands,
Now this, now that way glancing, to shake off
The heat still falling fresh. I thus begun :
     *   *   *   " Say, who
Is yon huge spirit, that, as seems, heeds not
The burning, but lies writhen in proud scorn,

As by the sultry tempest immatured ? "
Straight he himself, who was aware I ask'd
My guide of him, exclaim'd. " Such as I was
When living, dead such now I am. If Jove
Weary his workman out, from whom in ire
He snatch'd the lightnings, that at my last day
Transfix'd me, if the rest he weary out,
At their black smithy labouring by turns,
In Mongibello, while he cries aloud :
' Help, help, good Mulciber,' as erst he cried
In the Phlegræan warfare , and the bolts
Launch he, full aim'd at me, with all his might ,
He never should enjoy a sweet revenge."
Then, thus my guide, in accent higher raised
Than I before had heard him : " Capaneus !
Thou art more punish'd, in that this thy pride
Lives yet unquench'd : no torment, save thy rage,
Were to thy fiery pain proportion'd full."
     *   *   *   Silently on we pass'd,
To where there gushes from the forest's bound
A little brook, whose crimson'd wave yet lifts
My hair with horror.

CANTO XV.

PASSING along one of the mounds which form the embankment of the stream, Dante and Virgil come upon a troop of spirits, who, eyeing them, come beside the pier. They are the spirits of those who have broken Nature's laws. One of them catching at Dante's skirt he recognises as Brunetto Latini, his former tutor, with whom he discourses :—

One of the solid margins bears us now
Enveloped in the mist that, from the stream
Arising, hovers o'er, and saves from fire
Both piers and water.   *   *   *
     *   *   * We from the wood
Were now so far removed that, turning round,
I might not have discern'd it, when we met
A troop of spirits, who came beside the pier.
They each one eyed us, as at eventide
One eyes another under a new moon ;
And towards us sharpen'd their sight as keen
As an old tailor at his needle's eye.
Thus narrowly explored by all the tribe,
I was agnised of one, who by the skirt
Caught me and cried : " What wonder have we here ? "
And I, when he to me outstretch'd his arm,
Intently fix'd my ken on his parch'd looks,
That, although smirch'd with fire, they hinder'd not
But I remember'd him ; and towards his face
My hand inclining answer'd : " Ser Brunetto !

And are ye here ? " He thus to me : " My son !
Oh, let it not displease thee, if Brunetto
Latini but a little space with thee
Turn back, and leave his fellows to proceed.
I thus to him replied : " Much as I can
I thereto pray thee ; and, if thou be willing
That I here sent me with thee, I consent ;
His leave, with whom I journey, first obtain'd."
" O son," said he, " whoever of this throng
One instant stops, lies then a hundred years,
No fan to ventilate him when the fire
Smites sorest. Pass thou therefore on. I close
Will at thy garments walk, and then rejoin
My troop, who go mourning their endless doom."
     *   *   *   *   *
Thereat my sapient guide upon his right
Turn'd himself back, then look'd at me, and spake :
" He listens to good purpose who takes note."
I not the less still on my way proceed,
Discoursing with Brunetto.

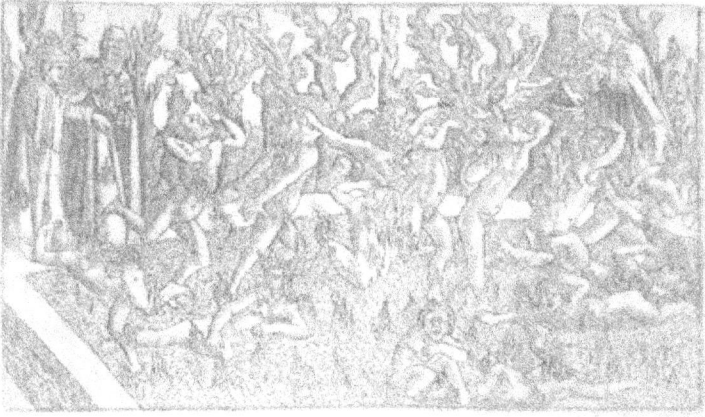

DANTE'S INFERNO—CANTO XVI.

PROCEEDING further along the mound the pair arrive near the end of the stream. Here Dante is accosted by three of the spirits of his countrymen Guidoguerra, Aldobrandi, and Rusticucci. Arriving where the stream descends into the eighth circle, Virgil throws into the abyss the girdle of Dante, which brings up from its depths a monster of hideous shape:—

Now came I where the water's din was heard,
As down it fell into the other round,
Resounding like the hum of swarming bees :
When forth together issued from a troop,
That pass'd beneath the fierce tormenting storm,
Three spirits, running swift. They towards us came,
And each one cried aloud : "Oh I do thou stay,
Whom, by the fashion of thy garb, we deem
To be some inmate of our evil land."

    *   *   *   *

" If woe of this unsound and dreary waste,"
Thus one began, "added to our sad cheer
Thus peel'd with flame, do call forth scorn on us
And our entreaties, let our great renown
Incline thee to inform us who thou art,
That dost imprint, with living feet unharm'd,
The soil of Hell? He in whose track thou see'st
My steps pursuing, naked though he be
And reft of all, was of more high estate
Than thou believest : grandchild of the chaste
Gualdrada, him they Guidoguerra call'd,
Who in his lifetime many a noble act

Achieved, both by his wisdom and his sword.
The other, next to me, that beats the sand,
Is Aldobrandi, name deserving well,
In the upper world, of honour ; and myself,
Who in this torment do partake with them,
Am Rusticucci."

    *   *   *   *

I had a cord that braced my girdle round,
Wherewith I erst had thought fast bound to take
The painted leopard. This, when I had all
Unloosen'd from me (so my master bade),
I gather'd up, and stretch'd it forth to him.
Then to the right he turn'd, and from the brink
Standing few paces distant, cast it down
Into the deep abyss. * * *
Through the gross and murky air I spied
A shape come swimming up, that might have quell'd
The stoutest heart with wonder ; in such guise
As one returns who hath been down to loose
An anchor grappled fast against some rock,
Or to aught else that in the salt wave lies,
Who, upward springing, close draws in his feet

CANTO XVII.

VIRGIL points out the monster Geryon, whom he beckons to him. Further on Dante beholds another tribe of spirits tormented for having done violence to Art. Each bears upon his breast an escutcheon with the emblems of a lion, a goose, and a swine, the arms respectively of the Gianfigliazzi, the Ubbriacchi, and the Scrovigni. After conversing with these Dante returns and finds Virgil seated on the back of the beast. Encouraged to do the like, Dante mounts, and they descend together towards the eighth circle :—

" Lo! the fell monster with the deadly sting,
Who passes mountains, breaks through fenced walls
And firm embattled spears, and with his filth
Taints all the world." Thus me my guide address'd,
And beckon'd him, that he should come to shore
Near to the stony causeway's utmost edge.

His face the semblance of a just man's wore,
So kind and gracious was its outward cheer ;
The rest was serpent all : two shaggy claws
Reach'd to the armpits ; and the back and breast
And either side were painted o'er with nodes
And orbits * * * In the void
Glancing, his tail upturn'd its venomous fork,
With sting like scorpion's arm'd.
    *   *   *   *
A little further on mine eye beholds
A tribe of spirits, seated on the sand.
    *   *   *   *
Noting the visages of some who lay
Beneath the pelting of that dolorous fire,
One of them all I knew not ; but perceived

That, pendent from his neck, each bore a pouch
With colours and with emblems various mark'd,
On which it seem'd as if their eye did feed.
And, when amongst them looking round I came,
A yellow purse I saw with azure wrought,
That wore a lion's countenance and port.
Then, still my sight pursuing its career,
Another I beheld than blood more red,
A goose display of whiter wing than curd,
And one who bore a fat and azure swine
Pictured on his white scrip.
    *   *   *   *
Backward my steps from those sad spirits turn'd,
My guide already seated on the haunch
Of the fierce animal I found.
    *   *   *   *
I settled me upon those shoulders huge.
    *   *   *   *
Soon as I mounted in his arms aloft,
Embracing hold me up ; and thus he spake :
"Geryon ! now move thee : be thy wheeling gyres
Of ample circuit, easy thy descent.
Think on the unusual burden thou sustain'st."

:

DANTE'S INFERNO—CANTO XVIII.

DESCENDING from Geryon's back at the foot of a rock in a region called Malebolge, near ten yawning chasms flanked with bridges, Dante sees in one of them the spirits of swarms of naked sinners being scourged by Demons. He catches sight of and accosts the spirit of Venedico Caccianimico. In another chasm he sees other spirits immersed in ordure, amongst whom, searching with inquisitive eye, he recognises Alessio and the courtezan Thais :—

There is a place within the depths of hell,
Call'd Malebolge, all of rock dark-stain'd
With hue ferruginous, e'en as the steep
That round it circling winds. Right in the midst
Of that abominable region, yawns
A spacious gulf profound, whereof the frame
Due time shall tell. The circle that remains,
Throughout its round, between the gulf and base
Of the high craggy banks, successive forms
Ten bastions in its hollow bottom raised.

    *   *   *   *

From Geryon's back dislodged, the bard to left
Held on his way, and I behind him moved.
On our right hand new misery I saw,
New pains, new executioners of wrath,
That swarming peopled the first chasm. Below
Were naked sinners. Hitherward they came.

    *   *   *   *

Each diverse way, along the grisly rock,
Horn'd Demons I beheld, with lashes huge,
That on their back unmercifully smote.

    *   *   *   *

Meantime, as on I pass'd, one met my sight,
Whom soon as view'd, "Of him," cried I, "not yet
Mine eye hath had its fill." I therefore stay'd
My feet to scan him, and the teacher kind
Paused with me, and consented I should walk
Backward a space ; and the tormented spirit,
Who thought to hide him, bent his visage down.
But it avail'd him naught ; for I exclaim'd :
"Thou who dost cast thine eye upon the ground,
Unless thy features do belie thee much,
Venedico art thou."

    *   *   Now had we come
Where, crossing the next pier, the straiten'd path
Bestrides its shoulders to another arch.
And thence I saw within the fosse below,
A crowd immersed in ordure, that appear'd
Draff of the human body. There beneath,
Searching with eye inquisitive, I mark'd
One with his head so grimed, 'twere hard to deem
If he were clerk or layman.   *   *
"And thou Alessio art, of Lucca sprung."

CANTO XIX.

DANTE and Virgil reach the third chasm, where those condemned for simony are punished by being fixed head downwards in circular pits, their legs only appearing : on the soles of their feet burning flames play continually. Dante, descending with his guide to the fourth pier, finds Pope Nicholas the Fifth, with whom he converses. Afterwards Virgil, catching Dante in his arms, carries him back to the arch leading to the fifth pier :—

Upon the following vault
We now had mounted, where the rock impends
Directly o'er the centre of the fosse.   *

    *   *   *   *

I saw the livid stone, throughout the sides
And in its bottom, full of apertures,
All equal in their width, and circular each.
    *   *   From out the mouth
Of every one emerged a sinner's feet,
And of the legs high upward as the calf.
The rest beneath was hid. On either foot
The soles were burning ; whence the flexile joints
Glanced with such violent motion, as had snaps
Asunder cords or twisted withs. As flame,
Feeding on unctuous matter, glides along
The surface, scarcely touching where it moves,
So here from heel to point glided the flames.

    *   *   *   *

Thereat on the fourth pier we came, we turn'd,
And on our left descended to the depth,

A narrow strait, and perforated close.
Nor from his side my leader set me down,
Till to his orifice he brought whose limb
Quiv'ring express'd his pang. "Whoe'er thou art,
Sad spirit ! thus reversed, and as a stake
Driv'n in the soil," I in these words began :
"If thou be able, utter forth thy voice."

    *   *   *   *

"What then of me requir'st ? If to know
So much imports thee who I am that thou
Hast therefore down the bank descended, learn
That in the mighty mantle I was robed,
And of a she-bear was indeed the son."

    *   *   In both arms
He caught, and to his bosom lifting me,
Upward retraced the way of his descent.
Nor weary of his weight he press'd me close,
Till to the summit of the rock we came,
Our passage from the fourth to the fifth pier.

THE TRIUMPH OF LOVE.

The Poet relates a vision he had at break of day at Vaucluse, in which he beheld Love seated on a chariot of fire drawn by four white horses, having Jupiter chained to the front of it, behind which followed a prodigious number of Love's prisoners, whose names he learns from a friend who is amongst them. In three other chapters the poet relates an interview he had with King Masinissa, Sophonisba, Seleucus, and Antiochus, and speaks of and names a great number of other lovers, and finally describes their triumphs and torments:—

It was the time when I do sadly pay
My sighs, in tribute to that sweet soft day,
Which first gave being to my tedious woes,
The sun upon the Bull's horns proudly goes,
And Phœbon had renew'd his scorce race;
When Love, the season, and my own ill case,
Drew me that solitary place to find
In which I oft unload my charged mind:
There, tired with roving thoughts and helpless moan,
Sleep seal'd my eyes up, and, its senses gone,
My waking fancy used a sleeping light,
In which appear'd long pain, and short delight.
A mighty General I then did see,
Like one who, for some glorious victory,
Should to the Capitol in triumph go:
I (who had not been used to such a show
In this soft age, where we no valour have,
But pride) observed his habit, strange and brave,
And having raised mine eyes, which seemed were,
To understand this sight was all my care.
Four snowy steeds a fiery chariot drew;
There sat the cruel boy; a threatening yew
His right hand bore, his other arrows bold,
Against whose force no helm or shield prevail'd.
Two party-colour'd wings his shoulders wore;
All naked else; and round about his chair
Were thousand mortals: some in battle ta'en,
Many were hurt with darts, and many slain.
Glad to learn news, I rose, and forward press'd
So far, that I was one amongst the rest;
As if I had been kill'd with loving pain
Before my time; and, looking through the train
Of this tear-thirsty king, I would have spied
Some of my old acquaintance, but descried
No face I knew, if any such there were,
They were transform'd with prison, death, and care.
At last one ghost, less sad than th' others came,
Who, near approaching, call'd me by my name,
And said: "This comes of Love." "What may you be,"
I answer'd, wondering much, "that thus know me?"
For I remember not t' have seen your face.
He thus replied: "It is the dusky place
That dulls thy sight, and this hard yoke I bear:
Else I a Tuscan am; thy friend, and dear
To thy remembrance." His wonted phrase
And voice did then discover what he was.
So we retired aside, and left the throng,
When thus he spake: "I have expected long
To see you here with us; your face did seem
To threaten you no less. I do esteem
Your prophecies; but I have seen what care
Attends a lover's life; and must beware."
"Yet have I oft been beaten in the field,
And sometimes hurt," said I, "but scorn'd to yield."
He smiled and said: "Alas! thou dost not see,
My son, how great a flame's prepared for thee."

I knew not then what by his words he meant:
But since I find it by the dire event;
And in my memory 'tis fix'd so fast,
That marble gravings cannot firmer last.
Meanwhile my forward youth did thus inquire:
"What may these people be? I much desire
To know their names; pray, give me leave to ask."
"I think ere long 'twill be a needless task,"
Replied my friend; "thou shalt be of the train,
And know them all; this captivating chain
Thy neck must bear (though thou dost little fear),
And sooner change thy comely form and hair,
Than be unfetter'd from the cruel tie,
Howe'er thou struggle for thy liberty,
Yet, to fulfil thy wish, I will relate
What I have learn'd. The first that keeps such state,
By whom our lives and freedoms we forego,
The world hath call'd him Love; and he (you know,
But shall know better when he comes to be
A lord to you, as now he is to me)
Is in his childhood mild, fierce in his age:
'Tis best believed of those that feel his rage.
The truth of this thou in thyself shalt find,
I warn thee now; pray keep it in thy mind."
Of idle looseness he is oft the child,
With pleasant fancies nourish'd and is styled
Or made a god by vain and foolish men:
And for a recompense, some meet their bane;
Others, a harder slavery must endure
Than many thousand chains and bars procure
That other gallant lord is conqueror
Of conquering Rome, led captive by the fair
Egyptian queen, with her persuasive art,
Who in his honours claims the greatest part;
For binding the world's victor with her charms,
His trophies are all hers by right of arms.
The next is his adoptive son, whose love
May seem more just, but doth no better prove;
For though he did his lovèd Livia wed,
She was seduced from her husband's bed.
Nero is third, disdainful, wicked, fierce,
And yet a woman found a way to pierce
His angry soul. Behold, Marcus, the grave
Wise emperor, is fair Faustina's slave.
These two are tyrants: Dionysius,
And Alexander, both suspicious,
And yet both loved: the last a just reward
Found of his causeless fear. I know y' have heard
Of him, who for Creüsa on the rock
Antandrus mourn'd so long; whose warlike stroke
At once revenged his friend and won his love:
And of the youth whom Phædra could not move
T' abuse his father's bed; he left the place,
And by his error lost his life (for base
Unworthy lovers to rage do quickly change);
It kill'd her too; perhaps in just revenge

---

* The lines in Italics are the rendering into English of the six lines in Italian at the foot of the print, the "Triumph of Love."

Of wrong'd Theseus, slain Hippolytus,
And poor forsaken Ariadne: thus
It often proves that they who falsely blame
Another, in one breath themselves condemn:
And who have guilty been of treachery,
Need not complain, if they deceived be.
Behold the brave hero a captive made
With all his fame, and 'twixt those sisters led:
Who, as he joy'd the death of th' one to see,
His death did ease the other's misery.
The next that followeth, though the world admire
His strength, Love bound him. Th' other fell of ice
Is great Achilles, he whose pitied fate
Was caused by Love. Demophoon did not hate
Impatient Phyllis, yet procured her death.
This Jason is, he whom Medea hath
Obliged by mischief; she to her father proved
False, to her brother cruel; t' him she loved
Grew furious, by her merit over-prized.
Hypsipyle comes next, mournful, despised,
Wounded to see a stranger's love prevail
More than her own, a Greek. Here is the frail
Fair Helena, with her the shepherd boy,
Whose gazing looks hurt Greece, and ruin'd Troy.

'Mongst other weeping souls, you hear the moan
Oenone makes, her Paris being gone;
And Menelaus, for the woe he had
To lose his wife. Hermione is sad,
And calls her dear Orestes to her aid.
And Laodamia, that hapless maid,
Bewails Protesilaus. Argia proved
To Polynice more faithful than the loved
(But false and covetous) Amphiaraus' wife.
The groans and sighs of those who lose their life
By this kind lord, in unrelenting flames
You hear: I cannot tell you half their names,
For they appear not only men that love,
The gods themselves do fill this myrtle grove:
You see fair Venus caught by Vulcan's art
With angry Mars: Proserpina apart
From Pluto, jealous Juno, yellow-hair'd
Apollo, who the young god's courage dared;
And, of his trophies proud, laugh'd at the bow,
Which in Thessalia gave him such a blow.
What shall I say?—here, in a word, are all
The gods that Varro mentions, great and small;
Each with innumerable bonds detain'd,
And Jupiter before the chariot chain'd."

Quella e colui chel mondo chiama amore
Amaro chome uedi & uedrai meglio
Quando fia tuo chome nostro signore.

E i nacque deſio & di la seſitia humana
Nutrio di penſier dolor & ſonni
Facto ſignor & dio da g ente uana.

PETRARCH'S TRIUMPHS.*

THE TRIUMPH OF CHASTITY.

The Poet relates the battle between Love and Chastity in the person of Laura, and describes the
victory and triumph of the latter, and the manner in which Chastity binds and leads Love prisoner to her
Temple at Rome accompanied by a troop of maids and chaste matrons, afterwards consecrating his bow
and arrows in memory of his defeat:—

When to one yoke at once I saw the height
Of gods and men subdued by Cupid's might,
I took example from their cruel fate,
And by their sufferings eased my own hard state ;
Since Phœbus and Leander felt like pain,
The one a god, the other but a man :
One snare caught Jove and the Carthage dame
(Her husband's death prepared her funeral flame—
'Twas not a cause that Virgil maketh one) ;
I need not grieve thus unprepared, alone,
Unsaved, and young, I did recover a wound,
Or that my enemy no hurt hath found
By Love ; or that she clothed him in my sight,
And took his wings, and reared his winding flight ;
No angry lions send more hideous noise
From their hot breasts, nor clashing thunder's voice
Rends heaven, frights earth, and roareth through the air
With greater force than Love had raised, to dare
Encounter her of whom I write ; and she
As quick and ready to assail as he :
Enceladus when Etna most he shakes,
Nor angry Scylla nor Charybdis makes
So great and frightful noise, as did the shock
Of this (first doubtful) battle : none could mock
Such earnest war ; all drew them to the height
To see what 'mated their hearts and dimm'd their sight.
Victorious Love a threatening dart did show
His right hand held ; the other bore a bow,
The string of which he drew just by his ear ;
No leopard could chase a frighted deer
(Free, or broke loose) with quicker speed than he
Made haste to wound ; fire sparkled from his eye.
I burn'd, and had a combat in my breast,
Glad I have her company, yet 'twas not best
(Methought) to see her lost, but 'tis in vain
T'abandon goodness, and of fate complain :
Virtue her servants never will forsake,
As now 'twas seen, she could resistance make :
No fencer ever better warded blow,
Nor pilot did to shore more wisely row
To shun a shelf, than with undaunted power
She waved the stroke of this sharp conqueror.
Mine eyes and heart were watchful to attend,
In hope the victory would that way bend
It ever did ; and that I might no more
Be barr'd from her ; as one whose thoughts before
His tongue hath utter'd them you well may see
Writ in his looks ; "Oh ! if you victor be,
Great sir," said I, "let her and me be bound
Both with one yoke ; I may be worthy found,
And will not set her free, doubt not my faith :"
When I beheld her with disdain and wrath
So fill'd, that to relate it would demand
A better muse than mine : her virtuous hand
Had quickly quench'd those gilded fiery darts,
Which, dipp'd in beauty's pleasure, poison hearts.
Neither Camilla, nor the warlike host
That cut their breasts, could so much valour boast ;
Nor Cæsar in Pharsalia fought so well
As she 'gainst him who pierceth coats of mail ;

All her brave virtues arm'd, attended there,
(A glorious troop !) and marchèd pair by pair :
Honour and Modesty first in rank ; the two
Religious virtues make the second row
(By those the other women doth excel) :
Prudence and Modesty, the twins that dwell
Together, both were lodged in her breast :
Glory and Perseverance, ever blest :
Fair Entertainment, Providence without,
Sweet Courtesy, and Pureness round about ;
Respect of credit, fear of infamy ;
Grave thoughts in youth ; and, what not oft agree,
True Chastity and rarest Beauty ; these
All came 'gainst Love, and this the heavens did please.
And every generous soul in that full height
He had no power left to bear the weight ;
A thousand famous prizes hardly gain'd
She took ; and thousand glorious palms obtain'd,
Shook from his hands ; the fall was not more strange
Of Hannibal, when Fortune pleased to change
Her mind, and on the Roman youth bestow
The favours he enjoy'd ; nor was he so
Amazed who frighted the Israelitish host—
Struck by the Hebrew boy, that quit his boast ;
Nor Cyrus more astonish'd at the fall
The Jewish widow gave his general :
As one that sickens suddenly, and fears
His life, or as a man ta'en unawares
In some base act, and doth the finder hate ;
Just so was he, or in a worse estate :
Fear, grief, and shame, and anger, in his face
Were seen : no troubled seas more rage : the place
Where huge Typhœus groans, nor Etna, when
Her giant sighs, were moved as he was then.
I pass by many noble things I see
(To write them were too hard a task for me),
To her and those that did attend I go :
Her armour was a robe more white than snow,
And in her hand a shield like his she bare
Who slew Medusa ; a fair pillar there
Of jasp was next, and with a chain (first wet
In Lethe flood) of jewels fitly set,
Diamonds, mix'd with topazes (of old
'Twas worn by ladies, now 'tis not), first hold
She caught, then bound him fast ; then such revenge
She took as might suffice. My thoughts did change :
And I, who watch'd him victory before,
Was satisfied he now could hurt no more.
I cannot in my rhymes the names contain
Of blessèd maids that did make up her train ;
Calliope nor Clio could suffice,
Nor all the other seven, for th' enterprise ;
Yet some I will insert may justly claim
Precedency of others. Lucrece came
On her right hand ; Penelope was by,
Those broke his bow, and made his arrows lie
Split on the ground, and pull'd his plumes away
From off his wings : after, Virginia,
Near her vex'd father, arm'd with wrath and hate,
Fury, and iron, and love, he freed the state

---

* The Italian lines at the foot of this print are contained in the " Triumph of Death," and the rendering of them will be found in that poem.

Facsimiles of Early Italian Engravings.   K

And her from slavery, with a manly blow;
Next were those barbarous women, who could show
They judged it better die than suffer wrong
To their rude chastity; the wise and strong—
The chaste Hebrean Judith follow'd these;
The Greeks that saved her honour in the seas;
With these and other famous souls I see
Her triumph over him who used to be
Master of all the world: among the rest
The vestal nun I spied who was so bless'd
As by a wonder to preserve her fame;
Next came Hersilia, the Roman dame
(Or Sabine rather) with her valorous train,
Who prove all slanders on that sex are vain.
Then, 'mongst the foreign ladies, she whose faith
T' her husband (not Æneas) caused her death;
The vulgar ignorant may hold their peace,
Her safety to her chastity gave place;
Dido, I mean, whom no vain passion led
(As fame belies her); last, the virtuous maid
Retired to Arno, who no rest could find,
Her friends' constraining power forced her mind.
The Triumph thither went where salt waves wet
The Baian shore eastward; her foot she set

There on firm land, and did Avernus leave
On the one hand, on th' other Sybil's cave;
So to Linternus march'd, the village where
The noble Africane lies buried; there
The great news of her triumph did appear
As glorious to the eye as to the ear
The fame had been; and the most chaste did show
Most beautiful; it grieved Love much to go
Another's prisoner, exposed to scorn,
Who to command whole empires seemed born.
Thus to the chiefest city all were led,
Entering the temple which Sulpicia made
Sacred; it drives all madness from the mind;
And chastity's pure temple next we find,
Which in brave souls doth modest thoughts beget,
Not by plebeians enter'd, but the great
Patrician dames; there were the spoils display'd
Of the fair victress; there her palms she laid,
And did commit them to the Tuscan youth,
Whose marring scars bear witness of his truth:
With others more, whose names I fully knew
(My guide instructed me), that overthrew
The power of Love: 'mongst whom, of all the rest,
Hippolytus and Joseph were the best.

E ra felice natura, e di sua legna   N el che la gente rumorosa, e forte
   In campo verde mi condusse bella donna   I suoi nati con festa, e con piacere
   Come sicura, in pace, el dillo regno.   Beato è ben chi ivi trova morte.

PETRARCH'S TRIUMPHS.

THE TRIUMPH OF DEATH.

The Poet relates how Chastity (Laura), returning from her triumph, encounters Death, represented as a woman of hideous mien, clothed in a black mantle. He states how he then saw in a great plain a vast number of dead of all nations, amongst them Popes, Kings, Emperors, &c., all naked and miserable. Death discourses on the vanities of the world. The Poet then tells how Death had triumphed over Laura whom he describes in Chapter II., as visiting him after death :—

The glorious Maid, whose soul to heaven is gone
And left the rest cold earth, she who was grown
A pillar of true valour, and had gain'd
Much honour by her victory, and chain'd
That god which doth the world with terror bind,
Using no armour but her own chaste mind ;
A fair aspect, coy thoughts, and words well weigh'd,
Sweet modesty to these gave friendly aid.
It was a miracle on earth to see
The bow and arrows of the deity,
And all his armour broke, who erst had slain
Such numbers, and so many captive ta'en ;
The fair dame from the noble sight withdrew
With her choice company,—they were but few,
And made a little troop, true virtue's rare,—
Yet each of them did by herself appear
A theme for poems, and might well incite
The best historian : *they bore a solute
Unspotted ermine, in a field of green,
About whose neck a topaz chain was seen
Set in pure gold ; their heavenly words and gait
Express'd them blest were born for such a fate.*
Bright stars they seem'd, she did a sun appear,
Who darken'd not the rest, but made more clear
Their splendour ; honour in brave minds is found :
This troop, with violets and roses crown'd,
Cheerfully march'd, when lo, I might espy
Another ensign dreadful to mine eye,—
A lady clothed in black, whose stern looks were
With horror fill'd, and did like hell appear,
Advanced, and said, " You who are proud to be
So fair and young, yet have no eyes to see
How near you are your end ; behold, I am
She, whom they, fierce, and blind, and cruel name,
Who meet untimely deaths ; 'twas I did make
Greece subject, and the Roman Empire shake ;
My piercing sword sack'd Troy, how many rude
And barbarous people are by me subdued ?
Many ambitious, vain, and amorous thought
My unsooth'd presence hath to nothing brought ;
Now am I come to you, while yet your state
Is happy, ere you feel a harder fate."
"On these you have no power," she then replied,
(Who had more worth than all the world beside,)
" And little over me ; but there is one
Who will be deeply grieved when I am gone,
His happiness doth on my life depend,
I shall find freedom in a peaceful end."
As one who glancing with a sudden eye
Some unexpected object doth espy,
Then looks again, and doth his own haste blame :
So in a doubting pause, this cruel dame
A little stay'd, and said, "The rest I call
To mind, and know I have o'ercome them all" :
Then, with less fierce aspect, she said, " Thou guide
Of this fair crew, hast not my strength assay'd,
Let her advise, who may command, prevent
Decrepit age, 'tis but a punishment ;

From me this honour thou alone shalt have,
Without or fear or pain, to find thy grave."
" As He shall please, who dwelleth in the heaven
And rules on earth, such portion must be given
To me, as others from thy hand receive,"
She answer'd then ; alas we might perceive
Millions of dead heap'd on th' adjacent plain ;
No verse nor prose may comprehend the slain
Did on Death's triumph wait, from India,
From Spain, and from Morocco, from Cathay,
And all the skirts of th' earth they gather'd were ;
Who had most happy lived, attended there :
Popes, Emperors, nor Kings, no ensigns wore
Of their past height, but naked show'd and poor.
Where be their riches, where their precious gems,
Their mitres, sceptres, robes, and diadems ?
O miserable men, whose hopes arise
From worldly joys, yet be there few so wise
As in those trifling follies not to trust ;
And if they be deceived, in end 'tis just :
*Ah ! more than blind, what gain you by your toil ?
You must return once to your mother's soil,
And after-times your names shall hardly know,
Nor any profit from your labour grow ;
All these strange countries by your warlike stroke
Submitted to a tributary yoke ,†*
The fuel erst of your ambitious fire,
What help they now ? The vast and bad desire
Of wealth and power at a bloody rate
Is wicked,—better bread and water eat
With peace ; a wooden dish doth seldom hold
A poison'd draught ; glass is more safe than gold.
But for this theme a larger time will ask,
I must betake me to my former task.
The fatal hour of her short life drew near,
That doubtful passage which the world doth fear.
Another company, who had not been
Freed from their earthly burden there were seen,
To try if prayers could appease the wrath,
Or stay th' inexorable hand, of Death.
That beauteous crowd convened to see the end
Which all must taste ; each neighbour, every friend
Stood by, when grim Death with her hand took hold,
And pull'd away one only hair of gold.
Thus from the world this fairest flower is ta'en
To make her shine more bright, not out of spleen
How many moaning plaints, what store of cries
Were utter'd there, when Fate shut those fair eyes
For which so oft I sung ; whose beauty burn'd
My tortured heart so long ; while others mourn'd,
She pleased, and quiet did the fruit enjoy
Of her blest life : " Farewell," without annoy,
" True saint on earth," said they ; so might she be
Esteem'd, but nothing bates Death's cruelty.
What shall become of others, since so pure
A body did such heats and colds endure,
And changed so often in so little space ?
Ah, worldly hopes, how blind you be, how base !

---

* Rendering of the lines in Italian at foot of the print " Triumph of Chastity."   † Rendering of the lines in Italian at foot of the print " Triumph of Death."

Facsimiles of Early Italian Engravings.

If since I bathe the ground with flowing tears
For that mild soul, who sees it, witness bears ;
And thou who read'st mayst judge she fetter'd me
The sixth of April, and did set me free
On the same day and month.   Oh! how the way
Of fortune is unsure ; none hates the day
Of slavery, or of death, so much as I
Abhor the time which wrought my liberty,
And my too lasting life ; it had been just
My greater age had first been turn'd to dust,
And paid to time, and to the world, the debt
I owed, then earth had kept her glorious state :
Now at what rate I should the sorrow prize
I know not, nor have heart that can suffice
The sad affliction to relate in verse.
Of these fair dames, that wept about her hearse ;
" Courtesy, Virtue, Beauty, all are lost ;
What shall become of us ? None else can boast
Such high perfection ; no more we shall
Hear her wise words, nor the angelical
Sweet music of her voice." While thus they cried,
The parting spirit doth itself divide

With every virtue from the noble breast,
As some grave hermit seeks a lonely rest :
The heavens were clear, and all the ambient air
Without a threatening cloud ; no adversaire
Durst once appear, or her calm mind affright ;
Death singly did herself conclude the fight ;
After, when fear, and the extremest plaint
Were ceased, th' attentive eyes of all were bent
On that fair face, and by despair became
Secure ; she who was spent, not like a flame
By force extinguish'd, but as lights decay,
And undiscerned waste themselves away :
Thus went the soul in peace ; so lamps are spent,
As the oil fails which gave them nourishment
In sum, her countenance you still might know
The same it was, not pale, but white as snow,
Which on the tops of hills in gentle flakes
Falls in a calm, or as a man that takes
Desired rest, as if her lovely sight
Were closed with sweetest sleep, after the sprite
Was gone. If this be that fools call to die,
Death seem'd in her exceeding fair to be.

The night—that follow'd the disastrous blow
Which my spent sun removed in heaven to glow,
And left me here a blind and desolate man—
Now far advanced, to spread o'er earth began
The sweet spring dew which harbingers the dawn,
When slumber's veil and visions are withdrawn ;
When, crown'd with oriental gems, and bright
As newborn day, upon my tranced sight
My Lady sighed from her starry sphere :
With kind speech and soft sigh, her hand so dear,
So long desired in vain, to mine she press'd,
While heavenly sweetness instant warm'd my breast :
" Remember her, who, from the world apart,
Kept all your course since known to that young heart."
Pensive she spoke, with mild and modest air
Seating me by her, on a soft bank, where,
In greenest shade, the beech and laurel met.
" Remember ? Ah ! how should I e'er forget ?
Yet tell me, idol mine," in tears I said,

" Live you ?—or dreamt I—is, is Laura dead ?"
" Live I ?   I only live, but you indeed
Are dead, and must be, till the last best hour
Shall free you from the flesh and vile world's power.
But, our brief leisure lest desire exceed,
Turn we, ere breaks the day already nigh,
To themes of greater interest, pure and high."
Then I : " When ended the brief dream and vain
That men call life, by you now safely pass'd,
Is death indeed such punishment and pain ?"
Replied she : " While on earth your lot is cast,
Slave to the world's opinions blind and hard,
True happiness shall ne'er your search reward ;
Death to the good a dreary prison opes,
But to the vile and base, who all their hopes
And cares below have fix'd, is full of fear ;
And this my loss, now mourn'd with many a tear,
Would seem a gain, and, knew you my delight
Boundless and pure, your joyful praise excite."

O occhi chauti allhor che be giouo
fum uenute allagran madre annui
che uene nostro a poia furenaci

Non aspettate/che la morte
Chome fa lapiu parte:che si certo
Infinita e lafchiera degli fiocchi.

PETRARCH'S TRIUMPHS.

THE TRIUMPH OF FAME.*

THE Poet describes a vision in which he sees Fame triumph over Death. He sees a long array of people marching on, being those whose deeds and works had carried their memories down to posterity. In the second and third chapters the Poet mentions the names of Greeks, Romans, Jews, Assyrians, and others who had acquired celebrity in war or government, or had been renowned in science, philosophy, poetry, medicine, &c. :—

WHEN cruel Death his paly ensign spread
Over that face, which oft in triumph led
My subject thoughts; and beauty's sovereign light,
Retiring, left the world immersed in night;
The Phantom, with a frown that chill'd the heart,
Seem'd with his gloomy pageant to depart,
Exulting in his formidable arms,
And proud of conquest o'er seraphic charms.
When, turning round, I saw the Power advance
That breaks the gloomy grave's eternal trance,
And bids the disembodied spirit claim
The glorious guerdon of immortal Fame.
Like Phosphor, in the sullen rear of night,
Before the golden wheels of orient light
He came. But who the 'tendant pomp can tell,
What mighty master of the corded shell
Can sing how heaven above accordant smiled,
And what bright pageantry the prospect fill'd.
I look'd, but all in vain: the potent ray
Flash'd on my sight intolerable day
At first; but to the splendour soon inured,
My eyes perused the pomp with sight assured.
True dignity in every face was seen,
As on they march'd with more than mortal mien;
And some I saw whom Love had link'd before,
Ennobled now by Virtue's lofty lore.
Cæsar and Scipio on the dexter hand
Of the bright goddess led the laurell'd band.
One, like a planet by the lord of day,
Seem'd o'er illumined by her splendid ray,
By brightness hid; for he, to virtue true,
His mind from Love's soft bondage nobly drew,
The other, half a slave to female charms,
Parted his homage to the god of arms
And Love's seductive power: but, close and deep,
Like files that climb'd the Capitolian steep
In years of yore, along the sacred way
A marshal squadron came in long array.
In ranges as they moved distinct and bright,
On every burganet that met the light,
Some name of long renown, distinctly read,
O'er each majestic brow a glory shed.
Still on the noble pair my eyes I bent,
And watch'd their progress up the steep ascent.
The second Scipio next in line was seen,
And he that seem'd the lure of Egypt's queen;
With many a mighty chief I there beheld,
Whose valorous hand the battle's storm repell'd.
Two fathers of the great Cornelian name,
With their three noble sons who shared their fame,
One singly march'd before, and, hand in hand,
His two heroic partners trod the strand.
The last was first in fame; but brighter beams
His follower flung around in solar streams.
Metaurus' champion, whom the moon beheld,
When his resistless spears the current swell'd
With Libya's hated gore, in arms renown'd

Was he, nor less with Wisdom's olive crown'd.
Quick was his thought and ready was his hand,
His power accomplish'd what his reason plann'd,
He seem'd with eagle eye and eagle wing,
Sudden on his premeditated scene to spring,
But he that follow'd next with step sedate
Drew round his foe the viewless snare of fate,
While, with consummate art, he kept at bay
The raging foe, and conquer'd by delay.
Another Fabius join'd the noble pair,
The Pauli and Marcelli famed in war
With them the twice in the friendly shade,
Whose public virtue quench'd his love of life
With either Brutus ancient Curius came,
Fabricius, too, I spied, a nobler mien
(With his plain russet gown and simple board)
Than either Lydian with his golden hoard.
Then came the great dictator from the plough;
And old Serranus show'd his laurell'd brow,
Marching with equal step Cornelius next,
Who, fresh and vigorous in the bright career
Of honour, sped, and never slack'd his pace,
Till Death o'ertook him in the noble race,
And placed him in a sphere of fame so high,
That other patriots fill'd a lower sky.
Then those ungrateful hands that seal'd his doom
Recall'd the banish'd man to rescue Rome.
Torquatus nigh, a sterner spectre stood,
His features all besmear'd with filial blood.
He childless to the shades resolved to go,
Rather than Rome a moment should forego
That dreadful discipline, whose rigid lore
Had spread their triumphs round from shore to shore
Then the two Decii came, by Heaven inspired,
Divinely bold, as when the foe retired
Before their Heaven-directed march, amazed,
When on the self-devoted men they gazed,
Till they provoked their fate. And Curtius nigh
As when to heaven he cast his opened eye,
And all on fire with glory's opening charms,
Plunged to the Shades below with clanging arms,
Lævinus, Mummius, with Flaminius show'd,
Like meaner lights along the heavenly road;
And he who conquer'd Greece from sea to sea,
Then mildly bade th' afflicted race be free.
Next came the dauntless envoy, with his wand,
Whose more than magic circle on the sand
The frenzy of the Syrian king confined:
O'erawed he stood, and at his fate repined.
Great Manlius, too, who drove the hostile throng
Prone from the steep on which his members hung,
(A sad reverse) the hungry vultures' food,
When Roman justice claim'd his forfeit blood.
Then Cocles came, who took his dreadful stand
Where the wide arch the foaming torrent spann'd,
Stemming the tide of war with matchless might,
And turn'd the heady current of the fight.

---

* The Italian lines at the foot of this print are contained in the poem the "Triumph of Time," and the rendering of these will be found in that poem.

Fac-simile of Early Italian Engravings.

And he that, stung with fierce vindictive ire,
Consumed his erring hand with hostile fire.
Duillius next and Catulus were seen,
Whose daring navies plough'd the billowy green
That laves Pelorus and the Sardian shore,
And dyed the rolling waves with Punic gore.
Great Appius next advanced in sterner mood,
Who with patrician loftiness withstood
The clamours of the crowd. But, close behind,
Of gentler manners and more equal mind,
Came one, perhaps the first in martial might,
Yet his dim glory cast a waning light;
But neither Bacchus, nor Alcmena's son
Such trophies yet by east or west have won;
Nor he that in the arms of conquest died,
As he, when Rome's stern foes his valour tried.
Yet he survived his fame. But luckier far
Was one that followed next, whose golden star
To better fortune led, and mark'd his name
Among the first in deeds of martial fame:
But cruel was his rage, and dipp'd in gore
By civil slaughter was the wreath he wore.
A less ensanguined laurel graced the head
Of him that next advanced with lofty tread,
In martial conduct and in active might
Of equal honour in the fields of fight.
Then great Volumnius, who expell'd the pest
Whose spreading ills the Romans long distress'd.
Rutilius Cassus, Philo next in sight
Appear'd, like twinkling stars that gild the night.
Three men I saw advancing up the vale,
Mangled with ghastly wounds through plate and mail:
Dentatus, long in standing fight renown'd,
Sergius and Scæva oft with conquest crown'd;
The triple terror of the hostile train,

On whom the storm of battle broke in vain.
Another Sergius near with deep disgrace
Marr'd the long glories of his ancient race,
Marius, then, the Cimbrians who repell'd
From fearful Rome, and Lybia's tyrant quell'd,
And Fulvius, who Campania's traitors slew,
And paid ingratitude with vengeance due.
Another nobler Fulvius next appear'd;
And there the Father of the Gracchi rear'd
A solitary crest. The following form
Was he that often raised the factious storm—
Bold Catulus, and he whom fortune's ray
Illumined still with beams of cloudless day;
Yet fail'd to chase the darkness of the mind,
That brooded still on loftier hopes behind.
From him a nobler line in two degrees
Reduced Numidia to reluctant peace.
Crete, Spain, and Macedonia's conquer'd lord
Adorn'd their triumphs and their treasures stored.
Vespasian, with his son, I next survey'd,
An angel soul in angel form array'd;
Nor less his brother seem'd in outward grace,
But hell within belied a beauteous face.
Then Nerva, who retrieved the falling throne,
And Trajan, by his conquering eagles known.
Adrian, and Antonine the just and good.
He, with his son, the golden age renew'd;
And ere they ruled the world, themselves subdued.
Then, as I turn'd my roving eyes around,
Quirinus I beheld with laurel crown'd,
And five succeeding kings. The sixth was lost,
By vice degraded from his regal post;
A sentence just, whatever pride may claim,
For virtue only feeds eternal Fame.

PETRARCH'S TRIUMPHS.

THE TRIUMPH OF TIME.

The Poet sees a band of mortals moving on as if disdaining Time's resistless power; he then reflects how Time overthrows all mortal things, and destroys the remembrance of them and of those whose achievements had almost made their names immortal, and he says that man should therefore place his hopes on a more solid foundation than a worldly one, seeing how swiftly and surely time passes away:—

Behind Aurora's wheels the rising sun
His voyage from his golden shrine began,
With such ethereal speed, as if the Hours
Had caught him slumb'ring in her rosy bowers.
With lordly eye, that reach'd the world's extreme,
Methought he look'd, when, gliding on his beam,
That winged power approach'd that wheels his car
In its wide annual range from star to star,
Measuring vicissitude ; till, now more near,
Methought these thrilling accents met my ear :—
" New laws must be observed if mortals claim,
Spite of the lapse of time, eternal fame.
Those laws have lost their force that Heaven decreed,
And I my circle run with fruitless speed ;
If fame's loud breath the slumb'ring dust inspire,
And bid to live with never-dying fire,
My power, that measures mortal things, is cross'd,
And my long glories in oblivion lost.
If mortals on yon planet's shadowy face,
Can match the tenor of my heavenly race,
I strive with fruitless speed from year to year
To keep precedence o'er a lower sphere.
In vain you flaming coursers I prepare,
In vain the watery world and ambient air
Their vigour feeds, if thus, with angels' flight
A mortal can o'ertake the race of light !
Were you a lesser planet, doom'd to run
A shorter journey round a nobler sun ;
Ranging among yon dusky orbs below,
A more degrading doom I could not know :
Now spread your swiftest wings, my steeds of flame,
We must not yield to man's ambitious aim.
With emulation's noblest fires I glow,
And soon that reptile race that boast below
Bright Fame's conducting lamp, that seems to vie
With my incessant journeys round the sky,
And gains, or seems to gain, increasing light,
Yet shall its glories sink in gradual night.
But I am still the same ; my course began
Before that dusky orb, the seat of man,
Was built in ambient air : with constant sway
I lead the grateful change of night and day,
To one ethereal track for ever bound,
And ever treading one eternal round."—
And now, methought, with more than mortal ire,
He seem'd to lash along his steeds of fire ;
And shot along the air with glancing ray,
Swift as a falcon darting on its prey ;
No planet's swift career could match his speed,
That seem'd the power of fancy to exceed.
The courier of the sky I mark'd with dread,
As by degrees the baseless fabric fled
That human power had built, while high disdain
I felt within to see the toiling train
Striving to seize each transitory thing
That fleets away on dissolution's wing ;
And soonest from the firmest grasp recede,
Like airy forms, with tantalizing speed.

O mortals ! ere the vital powers decay,
Or palsied eld obscures the mental ray,
Raise your affections to the things above,
Which time or fickle chance can never move.
Had you but seen what I despair to sing,
How fast his courser plied the flaming wing
With unremitted speed, the soaring mind
Had left his low terrestrial cares behind.
But what an awful change of earth and sky
All in a moment pass'd before my eye !
Now rigid winter stretch'd her brumal reign
With frown Gorgonean over land and main ;
And Flora now her gaudy mantle spread,
And many a blushing rose adorn'd her bed :
The momentary seasons seem'd to fleet
From bright solstitial dews to winter's driving sleet,
In circle multiform, and swift career :
A wondrous tale, untold to mortal ear
Before : yet reason's calm unbiass'd view
Must soon pronounce the seeming fable true,
When deep remorse for many a wasted spring
Still haunts the frighted soul on demon wing.
Fond hope allured me on with meteor flight,
And Love my fancy fed with vain delight,
Chasing through fairy fields her pageants gay.
But now, at last, a clear and steady ray,
From reason's mirror sent, my folly shows,
And on my sight the hideous image throws
Of what I am,—a mind eclipsed and lost,
By vice degraded from its noble post ;
But yet, e'en yet, the mind's elastic spring
Buoys up my powers on resolution's wing,
While on the flight of time, with rueful gaze
Intent, I try to thread the backward maze,
And husband what remains, a scanty space.
Few fleeting hours, alas ! have pass'd away,
Since a weak infant in the lap I lay ;
For what is human life but one uncertain day !
Now hid by flying vapours, dark and cold,
And brighten'd now with gleams of sunny gold,
That mock the gazer's eye with gaudy show,
And leave the victim to substantial woe :
Yet hope can live beneath the stormy sky,
And empty pleasures have their pinions ply ; *
And frantic pride exalts the lofty brow,
Nor marks the snares of death that lurk below.
Uncertain, whether now the shaft of fate
Sings on the wind, or Heaven prolongs my date.
I see my hours run on with cruel speed,
And in my doom the fate of all I read ;
A certain doom, which nature's self must feel
When the dread sentence checks the mundane wheel.
Go I court the smiles of Hope, ye thoughtless crew !
Her fairy scenes disclose an ample view
To brainless men. But Wisdom o'er the field
Casts her keen glance, and lifts her beamy shield
To meet the point of Fate, that flies afar,
And with stern vigilance expects the war.

---

* Rendering of the lines in Italian at foot of the print, the "Triumph of Time."

Perhaps in vain my admonitions fall,
Yet still the Muse repeats the solemn call ;
Nor can she see unmoved your senses drown'd
By Circe's deadly spells in sleep profound.
She cannot see the flying seasons roll
In dread succession to the final goal,
And sweep the tribes of men so fast away,
To Stygian darkness or eternal day.
With unconcern.—Oh ! yet the doom repeal
Before your callous hearts forget to feel ;
E'er Penitence foregoes her fruitless toil,
Or hell's black regent claims his human spoil.
Oh, haste ! before the fatal arrows fly
That send you headlong to the nether sky,
When down the gulf the sons of folly go
In sad procession to the seat of woe !
Thus deeply musing on the rapid round
Of planetary speed, in thought profound
I stood, and long bewail'd my wasted hours,
My vain afflictions, and my squander'd powers :
When, in deliberate march, a train was seen
In silent order moving o'er the green ;
A band that seem'd to hold in high disdain
The desolating power of Time's resistless reign :
Their names were hallow'd in the Muse's song,
Wafted by fame from age to age along,
High o'er oblivion's deep, devouring wave,
Where millions find an unrefunding grave.
With envious glance the changeful power beheld,
The glorious phalanx which his power repell'd,
And faster now the fiery chariot flew,
While Fame appear'd the rapid flight to rue,
And labour'd some to save. But, close behind,
I heard a voice, which, like the western wind,
That whispers softly through the summer shade,
These solemn accents to mine ear convey'd :—
" Man is a falling flower ; and Fame in vain
Strives to protract his momentaneous reign
Beyond his bounds, to match the rolling tide,
On whose dread waves the long Olympiads ride,
Till, led by time, the deep procession grows
And in long centuries continuous flows ;
For what the power of ages can oppose ?
Though Tempe's rolling flood, or Hebrus claim
Renown, they soon shall live an empty name.
Where are their heroes now, and those who led
The files of war by Xanthus' gory bed ?
Of Tuscan Tyber's more illustrious band,
Whose conquering eagles flew o'er sea and land?
What is renown?—a gleam of transient light,

That soon an envious cloud involves in night,
While passing Time's malignant winds diffuse
On many a noble name pernicious news.
Thus our terrestric glories fade away
Our triumphs past the pageants of a day ;
Our fields exchange their lords, our kingdoms fall,
And thrones are wrapt in Hades' funeral pall.
Yet virtue seldom gains what vice had lost
And oft the hopes of good desert are cross
Not wealth alone, but mental stores decay,
And, like the gifts of Mammon, pass away ;
Nor wisdom, wealth, nor fortune can withstand
His desolating march by sea and land ;
Nor prayers, nor regal power his wheels restrain,
Till he has ground us down to dust again.
Though various are the titles men can plead,
Some for a time enjoy the glorious meed
That merit claims ; yet unrelenting fate
On all the doom pronounces soon or late ;
And whatsoe'er the vulgar think or say,
Were not your lives thus shorten'd to a day,
Your eyes would see the consummating power
His countless millions at a meal devour."
And reason's voice my stubborn mind subdued ,
Conviction soon the solemn words pursued ;
I saw all mortal glory pass away,
Like vernal snows beneath the rising ray ,
And wealth, and power, and honour, strive in vain
To 'scape the laws of Time's despotic reign.
Though still to vulgar eyes they seem to claim
A lot conspicuous in the lists of Fame,
Transient as human joys ; to feeble age
They love to linger on this earthly stage,
And think it cruel to be call'd away
On the latest morn of life's disastrous day.
Yet ah ! how many infants on the breast
By Heaven's indulgence sink to endless rest !
And oft decrepit age his lot bewails,
Whom every ill of lengthen'd life assails.
Hence sick despondence thinks the human lot
A gift of fleeting breath too dearly bought
But should the voice of Fame's obstreperous blast
From ages on to future ages last,
E'en is the trump of doom,—how poor the prize
Whose worth depends upon the changing skies !
What time bestows and claims (the fleeting breath
Of fever) is but, at best, a second death,—
A death that none of mortal race can shun,
That wastes the brood of time, and triumphs o'er the sun. *

---

* Rendering of the Italian lines at the foot of the print "The Triumph of Fame."

C he piu dun giorno e hora mortale
Nubile breue fredda, & pien dnoia:
Che pur bella parceana nulla uale

C oli fuggendo il mondo seco uolue:
Ne mai fi pofa ne farefta o torna
Io ho chora condotta in pres se luc

THE TRIUMPH OF ETERNITY.

THE Poet, feeling that nothing on earth has a long duration, resolves to give himself up to God as the Sovereign Good on whom he should fix all his hopes. In the end he imagines to have seen Eternity triumph over Time, describing the end of the world, the judgment to come, and the state of Eternal Glory :—

WHEN all beneath the ample cope of heaven
I saw, like clouds before the tempest driven,
In sad vicissitude's eternal round,
Awhile I stood in holy horror bound ;
And thus at last with self-exploring mind,
Musing, I ask'd, "What basis I could find
To fix my trust?" An inward voice replied,
"Trust to the Almighty : He thy steps shall guide ;
He never fails to hear the faithful prayer,
But worldly hope must end in dark despair."
Now, what I am, and what I was, I know ;
I see the seasons in procession go
With still increasing speed ; while things to come,
Unknown, unthought, amid the growing gloom
Of long futurity, perplex my soul,
While life is posting to its final goal.
Mine is the crime, who ought with clearer light
To watch the winged years' incessant flight ;
And not to slumber on in dull delay
Till circling seasons bring the doomful day.
But grace is never slow in that, I trust,
To make the mind, before I sink to dust,
With those strong energies that lift the soul
To scenes unhoped, unthought, above the pole.
While thus I ponder'd, soon my working thought
Once more that ever-changing picture brought
Of sublunary things before my view,
And thus I question'd with myself anew :—
"What is the end of this incessant flight
Of life and death, alternate day and night ?
When will the motion on these orbs impress'd
Sink on the bosom of eternal rest?"
At once, as if obsequious to my will,
Another prospect shone, unmoved and still ;
Eternal as the heavens that glow'd above,
A wide resplendent scene of light and love.
The wheels of Phœbus from the zodiac turn'd ;
No more the nightly constellations burn'd ;
Green earth and undulating ocean roll'd
Away, by some resistless power controll'd ;
Immensity conceived, and brought to birth
A grander firmament, and more luxuriant earth
What wonder seized my soul when first I view'd
How motionless the restless racer stood,
Whose flying feet, with winged speed before,
Still mark'd with sad mutation sea and shore.
No more he sway'd the future and the past,
But on the moveless present fix'd at last ;
As at a goal reposing from his toils,
Like earth unclothed of all its vernal foils.
Unvaried scene ! where neither change nor fate,
Nor care, nor sorrow, can our joys abate ;
Nor finds the light of thought resistance here,
More than the sunbeams in a crystal sphere.
But no material things can match their flight,
In speed excelling far the race of light.
Oh ! what a glorious lot shall then be mine
If Heaven to me these nameless joys assign !
For there the sovereign good for ever reigns,

Nor evil yet to come, nor present pains ;
No baleful birth of time its inmates fear,
That comes the burthen of the passing year,
No solar chariot circles through the signs,
And now too near, and now too distant, shines ,
To wretched man and earth's devoted soil
Dispensing sad variety of toil.
Oh ! happy are the blessed souls that sing
Loud hallelujahs in eternal ring !
Thrice happy he, who late, at last shall find
A lot in the celestial climes assign'd !
He, led by grace, the auspicious ford explores,
Where, cross the plains, the wintery torrent roars ;
That troublous tide, where, with incessant strife,
Weak mortals struggle through, and call it life.*
In love with Vanity, oh ! doubly blind
Are they that final consolation find
In things that fleet on dissolution's wing,
Or dance away upon the transient ring
Of seasons, as they roll. No sound they hear
From that still voice that Wisdom's sons revere ;
No vestment they procure to keep them warm
Against the menace of the wintry storm ;
But all exposed, in naked nature lie,
A shivering crowd beneath the inclement sky,
Of reason void, by every foe subdued,
Self-ruin'd, self-deprived of sovereign good ;
Reckless of Him, whose universal sway,
Matter, and all its various forms, obey ;
Whether they mix in elemental strife,
Or meet in married calm, and foster life.
His nature baffles all created mind,
In earth or heaven, to fathom, or to find.
One glimpse of glory on the saints bestow'd,
With eager longings fills the hearts of God
For deeper views, in that abyss of light,
While mortals slumber here, content with night :
Though nought, we find, below the moon, can fill
The boundless cravings of the human will.
And yet, what fierce desire the fancy wings
To gain a grasp of perishable things ;
Although one fleeting hour may scatter far
The fruit of many a year's corroding care ;
Those spacious regions where our fancies roam,
Pain'd by the past, expecting ills to come,
In some dread moment, by the fates assign'd,
Shall pass away, nor leave a rack behind ;
And Time's revolving wheels shall lose at last
The speed that spins the future and the past ;
And, sovereign of an undisputed throne,
Awful eternity shall reign alone.
Then every darksome veil shall fleet away
That hides the prospects of eternal day :
Those cloud-born objects of our hopes and fears,
Whose air-drawn forms deluded memory bears
As of substantial things, away so fast
Shall fleet, that mortals, at their speed aghast,
Watching the change of all beneath the moon,
Shall ask, what once they were, and will be soon ?

* Rendering of the lines in Italian at foot of the print, the " Triumph of Eternity.'

The time will come when every change shall cease,
This quick revolving wheel shall rest in peace :
No summer then shall glow, nor winter freeze ;
Nothing shall be to come, and nothing past,
But an eternal now shall ever last.
Though time shall be no more, yet space shall give
A nobler theatre to love and live.
The wingèd courier then no more shall claim
The power to sink or raise the notes of Fame,
Or give its glories to the noontide ray :
True merit then, in everlasting day,
Shall shine for ever, as at first it shone
At once to God and man and angels known.
Happy are they who in this changing sphere
Already have begun the bright career
That reaches to the goal which, all in vain,
The Muse would blazon in her feeble strain :
But blest above all other blest is he
Who from the trammels of mortality,
Ere half the vital thread, ran out, was free,
Mature for Heaven ; where now the matchless fair
Preserves those features, that seraphic air,
And all those mental charms that raised my mind,
To judge of heaven while yet on earth confined.
That soft attractive glance that won my heart
When first my bosom felt unusual smart,
Now beams, now glories, in the realms above,
Fed by the eternal source of light and love.
Then shall I see her as I first beheld,
But lovelier far, and by herself excell'd ;
And I distinguish'd in the bands above
Shall hear this plaudit in the choirs of love :—
" Lo ! this is he who sung in mournful strains
For many years a lover's doubts and pains ;
Yet in this soul-expanding, sweet employ,
A sacred transport felt above all vulgar joy."
She too shall wonder at herself to hear
Her praises ring around the radiant sphere :
But of that hour it is not mine to know ;
To her, perhaps, the period of my woe
Is manifest ; for she my fate may find
In the pure mirror of the eternal mind.
To me it seems at hand a sure presage,
Devotes my rise from this terrestrial stage ;
Then what I gain'd and lost below shall lie
Suspended in the balance of the sky,
And all our anxious sublunary cares
Shall seem one tissue of Arachne's snares ;
And all the lying vanities of life,
The sordid source of envy, hate, and strife,
Ignoble as they are, shall then appear

Before the searching beams of truth severe ;
Then souls, from sense refined, shall see the fraud
That led them from the living way of God.
From the dark dungeon of the human breast
All direful secrets then shall rise confess'd,
In honour multiplied—a dreadful show
To hierarchies above, and saints below.
Eternal reason then shall give her doom ;
And sever'd wide, the tenants of the tomb
Shall seek their portions with instinctive haste,
Quick as the savage speeds along the waste.
Then shall the golden hoard its trust betray,
And they, that, mindless of that dreadful day,
Boasted their wealth, its vanity shall know
In the dread avenue of endless woe :
While they whom moderation's wholesome rule
Kept still unstain'd in Virtue's heavenly school,
Who the calm sunshine of the soul beneath
Enjoy'd, will share the triumph of the Faith.

These pageants five the world and I beheld,
The sixth and last, I hope, in heaven reveal'd
(If Heaven so will), when Time with speedy hand
The scene despoils, and Death's funereal wand
The triumph leads. But soon they both shall fall
Under that mighty hand that governs all,
While they who toil for true renown below,
Whom envious Time and Death, a mightier foe,
Relentless plunged in dark oblivion's womb,
When virtue seem'd to seek the silent tomb,
Spoil'd of her heavenly charms once more shall rise,
Regain their beauty, and assert the skies :
Leaving the dark sojourn of time beneath,
And the wide desolated realms of death.
But she will early seek these glorious bounds,
Whose long-lamented fall the world resounds
In unison with me. And Heaven will view
That awful day her heavenly charms renew,
When soul with body joins. Gehenna's strand
Saw me enroll'd in Love's devoted band,
And mark'd my toils through many hard campaigns
And wounds, whose scars my memory yet retains.
Blest is the pile that masks the hallow'd dust !—
There, at the resurrection of the just,
When the last trumpet with earth-shaking sound
Shall wake her sleepers from their couch profound ;
Then, when that spotless and immortal mind
In a material mould once more enshrined,
With wonted charms shall wake seraphic love,
How will the beatific sight improve
Her heavenly beauties in the climes above !

WYMAN AND SONS, PRINTERS, GREAT QUEEN STREET, LINCOLN'S INN FIELDS, LONDON, W.C.

www.ingramcontent.com/pod-product-compliance
Lightning Source LLC
Chambersburg PA
CBHW021525270326
41930CB00008B/1091